MOTORCYCLE GUYS

A history of motorcycles

in Hagerstown, Maryland

This book is intended for informative, educational, and historical benefits in furthering the understanding of the motorcycle community throughout the Washington County, Maryland area from its earliest beginnings to the present.

Walter Stoddard

Oct. 1, 1903 – July 2, 1931

Illustrations

Many of the clippings and much of the research for this book are from archives of *The Hagerstown Morning Herald* and *The Daily Mail*, the predecessors of todays consolidated **Herald-Mail** newspaper. Many records of our history only exist today due to local newspapers. Magazines were the best and often only source of motorcycle information for decades. Present day trends have been hard on all print media. Many have disappeared. Please support your hometown papers, and other print outlets wherever you live.

Many of the period race photos in this book are from the Bob Myers collection courtesy of David Sites. Most of the motocross photos and all the Antietam MC photos are courtesy of Andy and Jeff Delauder. All have been previously posted on the **"Antietam Motosport Park (1968-2003)"** Facebook site.

Several images appear courtesy of Google Maps web service. As well, that resource has been invaluable in identifying and pinpointing locations relevant to this project.

Several photos and much valuable information was graciously provided by Richard Lyons. The son of former Falls Church, Virginia Indian Dealer, Bob Lyons.

Contents

Motorcycles.

Motorcycles have existed for about 130 years, and they've been around Hagerstown almost as long. Motorcycles can be disturbing or almost religious, and everything in between. The history of motorcycles is the history of America from the horse drawn era to the present. It's a story that parallels and has been influenced by virtually every other element of the 20th century. But this book is not so much about motorcycles as it is people.

Like all history, it's the collective tale of the individual life events of regular people. In this case, regular people with a common interest. This is the story of motorcycles, in Washington County Maryland.

"Nowhere can a man find a quieter or more untroubled retreat

than in his own soul."

Marcus Aurelius

2

In the beginning.

Exactly when the motorcycle was invented is disputable. In the early period of motor vehicle development, the ideal or even preferred number of wheels had not been given much thought. Neither was exposure to the elements of much concern. Even an enclosed carriage was the same temperature inside as outside and the carriage was still driven by someone on the outside. Travel by horseback or walking, as most people did, was totally exposed to heat, cold, rain and snow in 1900. While the umbrella is 4,000 years old, even it was not used for anything but shade from the sun for over 3,700 years!

Gottlieb Daimler's 1885 wooden Reitwagen is often called the first motorcycle because of its two large, wagon-type wheels. Closer attention revels two additional, solid wood outrigger wheels looking very much like the training wheels on a child's first bike. The Reitwagen had a decidedly horse-like saddle and lacked most other motorcycle/bicycle elements such as its front wheel being attached to the frame by a non-raked fork. Of the many other experimental vehicles entering existence during this time, wheels could number from one to four or even more. Propulsion was by various sources from steam engines to

gasoline or kerosene powered engines in various configurations. There were even some failed attempts at battery powered electric vehicles. Three-wheelers were briefly popular, then disappeared until the 1930's. What is sometimes called "the first car," was built by Carl Benz. It had three wheels, but it also had a bench seat and steering wheel. It was more of a motorized wheelbarrow than it was a three wheeled motorcycle.

Joseph Brecht and Carl Benz

Into the early twentieth century, any self-propelled vehicle might be called a *"moto-cycle,"* regardless of the number of wheels. It was in 1893 though that Edward J. Pennington of Chicago patented a self-propelled vehicle with two wheels, handlebars, a bicycle-style seat, and a gasoline motor. Pennington's vehicle would be recognized by anyone today as what it is. Looking very much like a bicycle with one of the odd-looking motors invented by Pennington. What was truly notable about Pennington's invention is what he named it. Pennington called his machine a *Motorcycle* (note the *"r"*).

United States Patent Office.

EDWARD J. PENNINGTON, OF CHICAGO HEIGHTS, ILLINOIS, ASSIGNOR TO THE MOTOR CYCLE COMPANY, OF CHICAGO, ILLINOIS.

WHEELED VEHICLE.

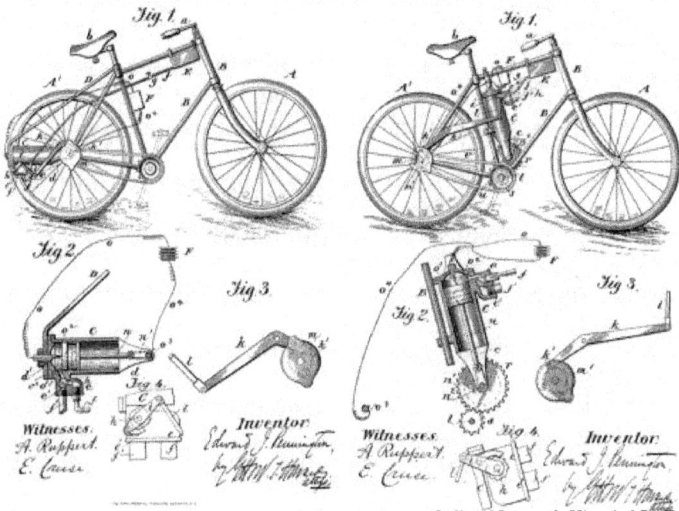

There were so many experimenters in so many places around the world working on a motor vehicle, it is questionable if we can name any single one of them as the first. E.J. Pennington though, *was* the first to coin the name that continues to describe these machines to the present.

Henri Fournier in Paris riding his De Dion powered two-wheeler. The similarities to Charles Metz's tandem Orient pacer built in Massachusetts the same year are unmistakable

Many of the earliest designs that would lead to modern motorcycles originally used French engines, or simply copied the design. The De Dion Bouton company sold a powerplant that was compact, lightweight, and powerful. Rather than keep it as a proprietary component for their own bikes, De Dion Bouton sold engines world-wide. Producing close to 140cc, the single cylinder engine while having its drawbacks, would incorporate many of the features used on motorcycle engines for more than 100 years.

Around the turn of the twentieth century, bicycles were enjoying a popularity that may not have been surpassed to the present. While the earliest motorcycles bear a strong resemblance to motorized bicycles, there is more to it than coincidence. Two wheelers, regardless of propulsion, share unique elements that make them stable. Early motorcycle experimenters leaned heavily on the lessons already learned by bicycle developers and the designs perfected over the preceding decades. Many of them were in both industries. Adding motorcycles to an existing bicycle business was a natural progression for numerous early companies.

Albert Pope's *"Pope Manufacturing"* had a large presence in Hagerstown. When Pope announced intentions to produce a motorcycle however, he chose to build the Pope "Model L" at his Massachusetts factory. But not only did successful motorcycle design grow out of the already proven design of bicycles, the first use of motorcycles for a utilitarian purpose rather than purely for pleasure was also most people's first exposure to them. That use was directly related to bicycle racing.

The initial success of motorcycles would not be as a means of transportation, but rather as an aid to bicycle racing. At the time "paced racing" was a popular practice to allow bicycle racers to go faster by creating a slipstream, or in racing terms a "draft" just ahead of the cycler. Originally, the pacer was another bicycle rider. To go fast enough to stay ahead of the racer, tandems, or bikes with multiple peddlers – as many as six - were employed. The addition of an engine assured the ability to go *just* faster than the racer with minimal effort.

The first time many people saw a motorcycle, or more correctly, *a cycle with a motor*, was one of these pacers at the popular bicycle races that toured the country annually. The date for the very first motorcycle in Hagerstown is unknown, but it may have been before 1900.

De Dion engine powered Orient Bicycle Company tandem pacer. The rider in front steers, the one in back operates the motor to maintain minimum separation with the cycler.

MADE NEW RECORD

Henry Smith, *who holds the Hagerstown-Balto. Record*, and his partner Tom Goode, on their motorcycle, the Southern Meteor, made another mark when they broke the mile record for the track at Tolchester in the Arlington Wheelmen's second annual meet. They established a new records of 3 minutes and 31 seconds, the best previous time for the mile on that track being 3 minutes and 43 seconds.

Hagerstown Daily Mail, June 16, 1900

[emphasis added]

Henry Smith and Tom Goode were clearly riding a tandem pacing bike. There are many other accounts of them doing so up and down the east coast. As races throughout Maryland were often promoted by the Baltimore club, it may explain why it is called the *"Hagerstown-Baltimore"* record. Hagerstown was then as well, Maryland's 2nd largest city. Clearly though, Smith and Goode had ridden the Hagerstown track *sometime* before June 1900 to have established a *Hagerstown* record. Races were then, and for many years afterward, held on the old "Great Hagerstown Fair" racetrack. This once prestigious raceway was ½ mile of a very wide racing surface that saw both horse and motor racing for many decades before World War II. By the following year, 1901, motorcycle racing was a genuine thing. Individual, single rider motorcycles racing each other instead of the clock.

Whitmonday

The roadrace on Whitmonday will be called at 1:30 p. m. and the track races of motorcycle, motor tandem, open and handicap races at 4 p. m. at the Fairgrounds.

Hagerstown Morning Herald, May 9, 1901

(*Whitmonday is the 7th week after Easter*)

The language in this brief article clearly differentiates between motorcycles and motor tandems. The announcement for the big Independence Day race later that summer gives more evidence. The motorcycles were still mostly a curiosity, but that would quickly change as the first technology revolution rapidly progressed. In less than a decade, motorcycle racing would eclipse the then enormous popularity of bicycle racing.

FOR THE MEET

Plans Progressing for the Big Gathering of Wheelmen

Sam. C. Miller, who is engertically working up the bicycle meet in Hagerstown July 2, 3, & 4, was at Harrisburg Tuesday to arrainge for several automobiles to be here during the meet and if possible to arrainge for a race between them.

Chariman Howard A. French, of the L.A.W. Race Committee is negotiating with Rhine of Washington; H. Fred Pompell, of Frederick, and Al Hoffberth and Will French of Baltimore to compete in a four-cornered motor paced race.

Joseph Parkin, the 11-year-old motorcyclist, Philadelphia, together with his brother, has entered.

Joseph Parkin has a postponed match race with Will French, in which race the latter will use Robert French's big motor, which was the first to break the Baltimore Electric Park record.

Harry Parkin will compete in the motorcycle handicap and will assist in pacing the five mile motor paced race.

Hagerstown Morning Herald, June 25, 1901

In 1897 George Hendee started a company in Middletown Connecticut to produce bicycles – the Silver Chief and Silver Queen. In 1900 he was joined by designer Oscar Hedstrom, both being former bicycle racers. In 1901 they built a proto-type motorcycle turning out 1 ¾

11

Oscar Hedstrom and his Indian

horsepower and by 1902, they began the first commercial sales of what they called the *Indian* brand of motorcycles. During the same period, three neighbors in Milwaukie Wisconsin were working on a similar project and in 1903, they began building the first *Harley-Davidsons*.

While Indian and Harley are the best known and longest lasting American motorcycle companies, they are by no means the only ones. In 1920 there were close to 100 motorcycle manufacturers in the United States. Fifteen years later, none would remain but Indian and Harley-Davidson. Of course, other experimenters around the world were building motorcycles to. Some of those brands remain or re-exist today as well.

> A Hagerstown man was in town with a motorcycle which made as much noise as a traction engine and can travel 60 miles an hour - "Chambersburg Repository" paper, Aug. 28, 1903

It is uncertain exactly when the first motorcycle came to Washington County. Early in their histories, both Indian and Harley-Davidson, as well as other maker's sales were from their respective factories. Frequently by mail order. Bikes were then shipped to the anxious buyer wherever he lived. Harley-Davidson is known to have begun establishing independent dealers around the country in 1909. By that time, Murray Brish in nearby Frederick, was already well established as an Indian dealer. In fact, we have documentation of Mr. Brish selling an Indian to a Hagerstown resident in 1905. By 1910 John Rowland could get his Indian motorcycle serviced without traveling to Frederick. John Connor and Ned Lambert would both

An Auto Trade

John Rowland, Hagerstown, traded a one-cylinder Covert automobile for an Indian motor cycle with Murray Brish, Frederick.

The Frederick Evening News 1905

eventually move into other fields, but their initial business venture, while both were in their 20's, was selling Indian motorcycles. Indian rider John Rowland's motorcycle interest would be long lasting as well.

HAVE AGENCY HERE

Ned E. Lambert and John Connor have secured the agency for the Indian motorcycle in Hagerstown and have one of the machines on exhibition in Gelback's cigar store window. The machine is a four-horse-power motor cycle and very attractive in appearance. Both of the young men are experienced motorists.

I have several photos from this event at the Great Hagerstown Fairground, from *about* 1920. Surprisingly, the camera shutter speed is fast enough to capture an amazingly crisp image. Unfortunately, the photographer's trigger finger was not as fast. The other photos are nothing but the trailing dust, with no motorcycle at all. Note the sidecar passenger laying on his side to reduce wind resistance, and still wearing his hat!

By 1908 motorcycle popularity, and dependability, had advanced to the point that nowhere was too far for a casual adventure. Distant cities were suddenly within reach of a daytrip, termed "Gypsy Tours." Multiple tourist sites that would have previously required individual trips could be tied together by a circular route and visited in a single day. Some gypsy tours included overnight camps. Motorcyclists can still relate that the route between the sites would have been as much a part of the adventure as the destinations themselves.

15

ROAD FLYERS TO GO OVER STATE

Motor Cyclists, of Baltimore Are Scheduled to Arrive Here At Noon Today.

The first long run ever held in this State on motor-cycles will begin this morning at 5 o'clock from the corner of Fulton avenue and Lanvale street, Baltimore.

Cumberland will be the destination of the party, and so far the following are sure to take part Capt. W. S. Fisher, 3½ horse power Indian; Howard A. French, 3½ horse power Indian; W. Rayner Straus, 5 horse power Indian; H. Mathew Gault, 5 horse power Indian, and George C. Willis, 2½ horse power Indian.

The trip has been and is still the absorbing topic of conversation in motorcycle circles. Those who take part in it will have a couple of days out in the open, breathing the fresh mountain air.

First Stop Ridgeville.

Leaving at daybreak this morning the first stop will be Ridgeville, where breakfast will be eaten. Hagerstown will be reached by noon if the schedule is followed:

No attempt will be made to speed, nor is the thought of an endurance run in the minds of the riders. It is their intention to go anywhere they may decide after being on the road, stop anywhere they may be to sleep and take their meals at any convenient place. There are several intermediate objective points in view— Hagerstown, Harper's Ferry, Frederick—and side trips will be taken to the different points of interest wherever good roads may lead.

Both W. Rayner Straus, and Howard French are familiar with the Western Maryland roads. The first named toured over the same roads only a few days ago, while French has many bicycle centuries to his credit over almost the same route.

Hagerstown Morning Herald, April 19, 1908

Sometimes mislabeled, this photo depicts an outing by the *Hagerstown Motorcycle Club* at the SE corner of Public Square in 1918 as O. Milton Wilhide described it when he furnished the photo for a Herald Mail article in 1955. Wilhide stated that the club and their Sunday tours were sponsored by Ned Lambert's Harley-Davidson shop.

16

TOOK A LONG TRIP.

Mr. Charles M. Lamar took a long trip on his motorcycle from Martinsburg. He started out at 9:30 in the morning, going from there to Shepherdstown, thence to Sharpsburg, to Boonsboro and half way up South mountain. He came back down the mountain and back to Sharpsburg for dinner. He left Sharpsburg at twenty minutes after one o'clock and made the trip from there to Hagerstown in twenty-five minutes. In Hagerstown one of his tires was punctured and he had to stop to have it fixed and his gasoline tank filled. He left Hagerstown five minutes of three o'clock and arrived at Martinsburg at 4:30, stopping to ferry the river at Williamsport and to pay toll at three toll gates on the way.

Hagerstown Daily Mail, September 22, 1902

Motorcycles did not enjoy a completely carefree integration into local society. Any number of archival news stories tell of conflicts. Particularly troublesome were the temperamental horses which remained the primary mode of transportation during the first couple decades of the new century.

There is a popularly cited comment from a prominent writer during the first decade of the 20th century which

17

described the motorcycle and rider as *"a bicycle with a pandemonium device attached to it operated by a man who is half dare devil, and half mechanical genius."* For anyone who has tried to ride one, or have the process explained to them or watched others operating them, this description of pre-1920 bikes and their operation turns out to not be too far off the mark.

As wildly popular as motorcycle racing was as a spectator sport, the machines and those who rode them were, from the very beginning, viewed as a different sort. The machines, little more than painful accidents in waiting. Unnecessary, noisy intrusions into and disruptions of *"normal"* civil life.

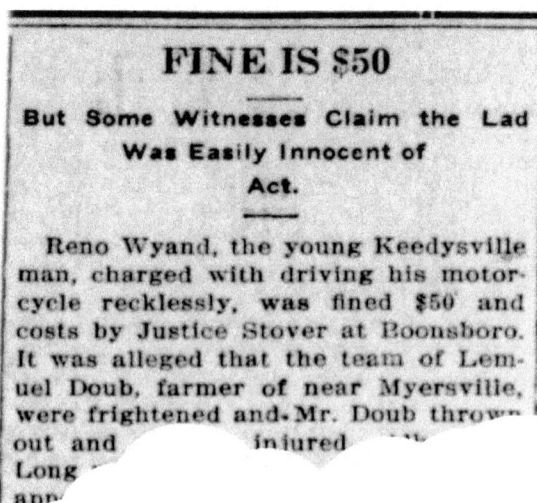

FINE IS $50

But Some Witnesses Claim the Lad Was Easily Innocent of Act.

Reno Wyand, the young Keedysville man, charged with driving his motorcycle recklessly, was fined $50 and costs by Justice Stover at Boonsboro. It was alleged that the team of Lemuel Doub, farmer of near Myersville, were frightened and-Mr. Doub throw~ out and   injured   ~ ``
Long
an~

April 10, 1914

IN CONVULSIONS

Mrs. Clinton Trovinger Has Exciting Experience in Locust Street.

Contractor Clinton Trovinger, South Locust street, and his wife were driving in a buggy in South Locust street, between Washington and Antietam streets, last night about 8 o'clock, when his horse was frightened by a motor-cycle and attempted to run away. Mr. Trovinger saw the cyclist approaching when he was some distance away and called to him to shut off the puffing noise, but this, Mr. Trovinger says, the rider of the machine failed to do. Mr. Trovinger jumped out of the buggy and grabbed the horse by the bridle, but as the motor-cycle got nearer the animal began to kick. The dash and bar in front of the buggy were broken and further damage was only averted by the horse getting its both legs over the single tree. A. T. Zentmyer, Frank L. Recher and others hastened to Mr. Trovinger's assistance. Mrs. Trovinger was taken from the buggy and carried into the home of Mr. Recher, where she was in convulsions for over half an hour. The horse's one leg was lacerated.

Mr. Trovinger stated after the occurrence that he would today swear out a warrant for the motor cyclist for immoderate riding.

Hagerstown Morning Herald, Sept. 23, 1902

HURT IN RUNAWAY.

Simon Sheffler's Horse Frightened By Motorcycle on the Pike.

Simon Sheffler, while driving by Mount Union, along the Leitersburg pike, toward Hagerstown Sunday afternoon in a falling-top buggy, with Harry Hartman, was thrown out of the buggy and severely hurt, the horse taking fright at a motorcycle that was coming behind. The motorcycle was ridden by a young man, a stranger to Mr. Sheffler and Mr. Hartman. The horse made a sudden turn, upset the buggy and threw out the occupants. Mr. Sheffler landed on his head against the fence and was rendered unconscious. Mr. Hartman was not hurt. The horse ran away. The buggy was badly broken. The horse was caught by Harry Martin. The cyclist stopped and went for help. After Mr. Sheffler revived he was assisted to the house of John Baumgartner, where he remained until his sons came and took him to his home, on the Hamilton farm, near Bellevue, where he was attended by a physician.

Hagerstown Morning Herald, Oct. 22, 1907

19

But motorcycles did become entrenched in Washington County just as they did throughout the world. Ned Lambert, who was previously noted together with John Conner as obtaining a dealership for Indian motorcycles in 1910, was by 1914, also Hagerstown's first Harley-Davidson dealer.

In 1915 Lambert appears to have incurred some problems. Or perhaps he was trying to raise capital for a different project. What is known is that several ads appear

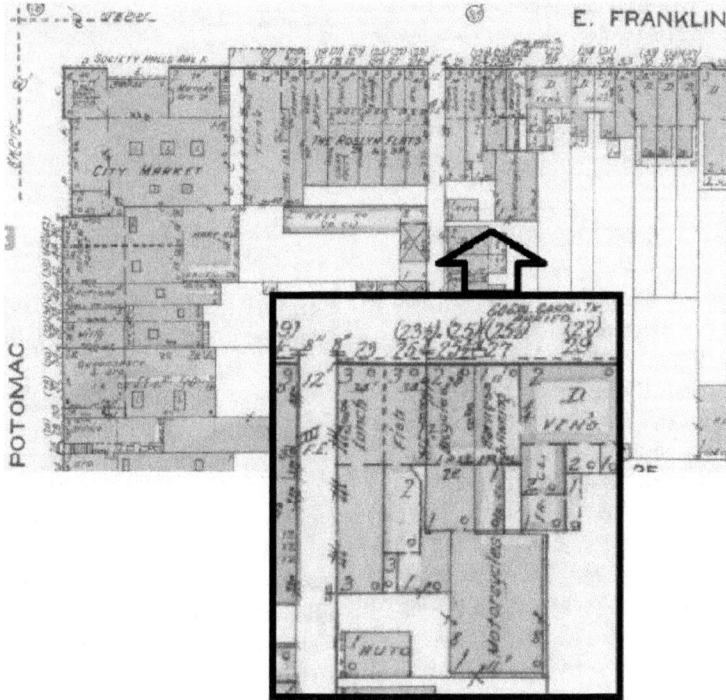

Ned Lambert's bicycle and motorcycle shop with curbside gasoline pumps on E. Franklin Street in 1918.

in the local paper in a short period of time offering various motorcycles for quick *cash* sale. The bikes offered include Indians and Harley's as well as others. Rather than a sale it appears more of a liquidation. Conner is not mentioned.

FOR SALE   MOTORCYCLE   1915
Three speed Harley - Davidson and sidecar motorcycle. All necessary equipment. Bargain for cash buyer. Good reasons for selling.
LAMBERT'S MOTORCYCLE SHOP.

Later the same year, 1915, Samuel Haines took over the Indian Dealership moving it to 27 West Antietam Street. There is some evidence that Haines may have been a relative of Lambert. Haines' mother's maiden name was Lambert, but the trail goes cold beyond there.

MOVES HIS SHOP

Samuel B. Haines Now In His New Location.

Samuel B. Haines has finished moving from his temporary quarters in Court Place to his handsome new shop in the Rauth Building, 27 West Antietam street. Mr. Haines, who has been engaged in the repair business for the past four years, has increased the capacity of his plant by the installation of power machinery.

Mr. Haines has the agency for the Indian motorcycle and has just received and ⸳ for inspectio⸳

While business was understandably centered in Hagerstown, motorcycles were popular throughout the county. One of my few memories of my grandfather Fred Wilhide, is a story he once told about the old gentleman who lived next door to my childhood home.

My grandfather told of being with a group of other young men sitting in front of the general store in Keedysville about 1912 when a loud unrecognizable noise and cloud of dust approached like a miniature cyclone down the unpaved street. The frightening commotion ceased right in front of them and as Papa told it, "...*when the dust settled, there sat Dave Kretzer on a motorsickle.*"

I unfortunately never got to ask Dave about his early motorcycle days. In failing health, he had moved away to live with relatives by the time I got *my* first motorcycle. Dave was a close, friendly, but outspoken neighbor with no qualms about sharing his thoughts. I can only imagine Dave's reaction had he seen me riding the little bike around the backyard right under the porch swing where he spent most of his time while I knew him.

Many years later, when Dave's old, dilapidated garage was torn down, I discovered a treasure there in the debris. A chain-breaker tool used to repair motorcycle chains.

Forged into the steel handle is the name, "HARLEY-DAVIDSON." Finally, I had gained some small glimpse into old Dave's early motorcycle days.

Dave's chain breaker

From the other end of the county, a report in the Frederick News on October 22, 1910, told about the motorcycle races held at The Great Frederick Fair the previous day. It noted that ***"H.E. Floerkeny, of Clear Spring, Maryland"*** was one of the top competitors.

W. Guy Lefevre of Hagerstown on a 1910 Marsh-Metz 1000cc 90-degree V-twin.   Charles Metz's first motorcycles in 1898 were the De Dion powered Orient tandem pacers pictured elsewhere. Guy Lefevre's grandson's, Jeff & Andy DeLauder would one day be major forces behind Hagerstown's moto cross park and Antietam MC.

Marsh-Metz motorcycle ad from "Cycle and Automobile Trade Journal

Ned Lambert's shop was at 33 E. Franklin Street. The motorcycle shop was in the rear. Today the site is in the city of Hagerstown's Franklin Street parking lot.

Whatever precipitated the apparent sell-off of Ned Lambert's stock of motorcycles, and the separation of the Indian brand from his stewardship, Ned did continue in the motorcycle and bicycle business. In fact, he retained the Harley-Davidson franchise for several more years to come and appears to have made quite a success in that venture.

Motorcycle Owners Guests At Banquet

Sixty-five local motorcycle owners and ladies were guests last night at a banquet given by Ned Lambert, proprietor of Lambert's Motorcycle Shop, East Franklin street. A delicious menu was served and Wagoner's orchestra furnished music during the evening.

Flashlight pictures of the banqueters were taken by a photographer from Heidwohl's Studio. The banquet was prepared by Mr. and Mrs. Ned Lambert, Mrs. Hallie K. Lambert, Wilbur Thomas and Robert Wright. Each lady received a carnation and the gentlemen were presented with Harley-Davidson pins and smokes.

April 5, 1923

Gatherings of motorcyclists used to look a bit different.

1920's Lambert customer banquet

Business was apparently good. In April 1924, Ned Lambert was issued a building permit for a new, modern, four-story apartment building at 31-33 E. Franklin. The building remains today with (as designed) several businesses at the street level and apartments on the upper three floors.

By 1925, what had become an annual spring banquet included 80 (named) attendees. It would however be Ned's last Harley-Davidson gala. At least as sponsor. By autumn, Ned sold his Harley-Davidson business to Chester and Ray Delphey from Frederick, Maryland. Chester would move to Hagerstown, where he'd live the rest of his life.

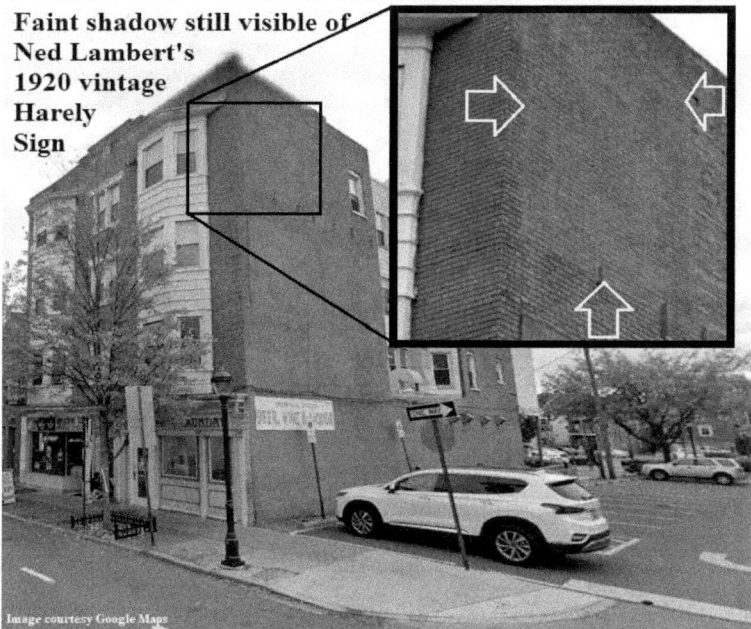

Faint shadow still visible of Ned Lambert's 1920 vintage Harely Sign

Image courtesy Google Maps

Evidence of Ned Lambert's devotion to motorcycles would be apparent for many more years, but in 1925, he appears to have had other prospects for business.

Oldsmobile Dealer Here Is Announced

The Olds Motor Co. announced today the appointment of The Lambert-Thomas Motor Co., as local dealers for the Oldsmobile motor cars.

The members of the Lambert-Thomas Co. are well known in this community. Mr. N. E. Lambert has been in business here for the past fourteen years. He was formerly the local agent for Harley-Davidson motorcycles and was one of the pioneer motorcycle men in the city. Mr. Lambert also represents the Goodyear Tire and Rubber Co.

Mr. W. C. Thomas is well known in automotive circles here and for the past three years has been connected with the Buick agency.

The new dealers will carry a representative line of Oldsmobile models. They will also maintain a complete stock of parts to meet the needs of every Oldsmobile owner.

The garage and showroom of The Lambert-Thomas Motor Co. is located at 33 East Franklin street.

In March 1928 not Ned Lambert, but the Oldsmobile Motor Company, made the announcement that Ned and his long-time friend Wilbur Thomas would be opening a new Oldsmobile dealership at the old motorcycle shop on

Franklin Street. During a snowstorm in January 1931, Ned and his pal Hagerstown police officer John Knode, caused quite a stir around town with what was undoubtedly the first "snowmobile" in the area.

Ned Lambert and John Knode were out in a motor bobsled and attracting lots of attention.

While difficult to discern details due to exposure issues with the photo, this is thought to be Ned & John's Harley powered motorsled. Note snow outside garage and chains on the rear wheel.

By 1931, it appears the great depression was taking a toll on business. In July Ned sold the Oldsmobile dealership to John Snowberger of Waynesboro, Pennsylvania. The business stayed on Franklin Street until moving to 35 W. Washington St. in August. Ned continued the repair business behind the storefront and apartment building he owned on Franklin Street and tried to reassure established customers.

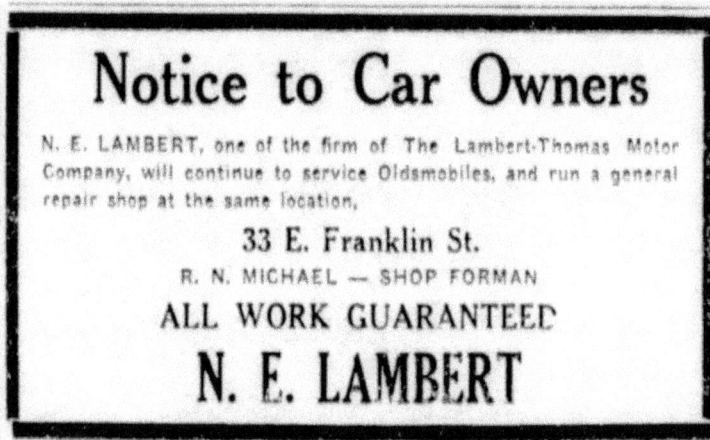

Notice to Car Owners

N. E. LAMBERT, one of the firm of The Lambert-Thomas Motor Company, will continue to service Oldsmobiles, and run a general repair shop at the same location,

33 E. Franklin St.

R. N. MICHAEL — SHOP FORMAN

ALL WORK GUARANTEED

N. E. LAMBERT

By 1933, Ned Lambert finally got back on solid financial ground thanks to President Franklin Roosevelt when as the old song goes, *"Happy days are here again…"* In February 1933 congress had voted to repeal prohibition, but alcohol sales had been banned by a constitutional amendment. Legalization would require it to be ratified by the majority of the individual state's legislatures.

That would take months. In the interim, a thirsty congress passed the Cullen-Harrison Act, and an equally thirsty Roosevelt signed it the next day! Cullen-Harrison made it legal to sell "low alcohol" (3.2%) beer and wine while waiting on ratification. The act became law on what has since been proclaimed *"National Beer Day,"* April 7th, 1933.

The above ad for Ned Lambert's yet unnamed bar and restaurant appeared on *April 7th, 1933*, the 1st day beer became legal to sell. Later named Lambert's Café, the first motorcycle shop in 1910, thus became the first post-prohibition beer joint in 1933. Ned and Ethel would run the café the rest of their lives. After Ned's death in 1956, it continued many more years under son in-law Bill White. Today, the location remains a packaged liquor store.

Photo of a young Ned (center) and some friends.

LAMBERTS CAFE

1960's era advertising thermometer

By 1921 John Conner was back in the Indian business. In 1917 Conner and his wife Mary bought lot #1 in what was then a brand-new housing development named *"Roe's Addition to Hagerstown."* The development was located on what was then still the Sharpsburg Pike and on the edge of town. Beside lot number one, squeezed between it and the then very busy B&O Railroad crossing was a tiny triangular lot that was too small for a house. John Conner, however, appears to have already envisioned his plans for the spot.

Conner's new, modern motorcycle shop beside the house where he'd spend the rest of his days would become 775 S. Potomac Street. It has been known from 1959 until 2018 as **Startzman's Hardware Store.** In the 1970's I worked for R.D. McKee's wholesale business in Hagerstown. One day while making a delivery at the store,

I overheard an elderly customer mention to long-time Startzman's clerk Charlie Ridenour, that the building had once been a motorcycle shop. I suppose it was only the oddity of that revelation that caused me to retain the memory all these years. The 1918 Sanborn map and Maryland land records tell the rest of the story. Like Lamberts, John Conner's shop included curbside gasoline sales for customer convenience.

As a poignant reminder of more recent events, John Conner's first wife, Mary, died at only 26 years during the Spanish flu pandemic in October 1918. It has been a hauntingly regular footnote throughout this research. John Conner, Chester Delphey, John Knode, and more lost their first and in some cases only wives during the outbreak a century ago before today's understanding of transmission and prevention measures.

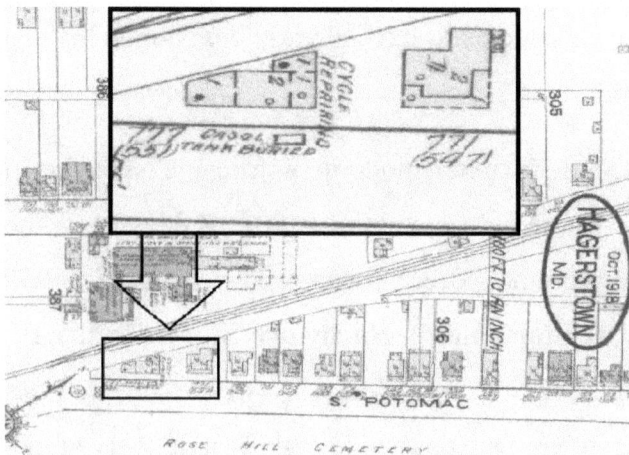

July 21, 1932

A stop during a 1920's group ride of N.E. Lambert customers.

Photo of John Knode hauling Ned and his boat on a modified sidecar behind the shop on E. Franklin Street. Ned is almost as well known in news reports as an avid, and very successful fishermen as he is a motorcyclist.

Know Your Policemen

Patrolman John A. Knode, a member of the traffic division of the Police Department since October 7, 1931, "worked on" the first motorcycle owned by the city in 1916.

Born in the Clearspring district May 2, 1889, Knode came to Hagerstown in 1912 to work on the round house and machine shop which was then being built by the Western Maryland Railway. Later he worked two years for the State Roads Commission and in 1915 became a mechanic for Ned Lambert, the motorcycle dealer. He worked at that job for the next 15 years with the exception of a brief interlude of eight months spent in the Army in 1918.

Patrolman Knode, a motorcycle policeman, once was responsible for the capture of a thief who stole a police cruiser from in front of headquarters in which the driver had conveniently left the keys. Knode caught the thief several miles out the Western Pike.

One of the regular jobs of a motorcycle policeman is to lead funeral processions and Knode said "I've led more processions than I care to remember."

In recent years his chief duties have been the repair of motorcycles, police cruisers and radio equipment which places him more in the class of a master mechanic than a policeman. Almost any day he can be found in the basement of City Hall with grease-blackened hands and shirt repairing a piece of police motor equipment.

Patrolman Knode, who is widower, his wife having been the first Hagerstown victim of the flu epidemic in 1918, resides at the Hotel Patterson. He has one daughter.

He is a member of the Jr. O. U. A. M., American Legion, 40 and 8, Eagles, Junior Fire Company and the Alsatians.

Tomorrow—Patrolman Lester J. Britcher.

1946 bio for long-time Ned Lamber friend John Knode.

Ned Lambert

AGENCY BOUGHT

Chester L. Delphey and Ray G. Delphey of Frederick, have purchased the Harley-Davidson Motorcycle Agency formerly conducted here by M.E. Lambert, at 33 East Franklin Street. The Delphey's will move into the Jamison building on West Franklin Street with their agency. They will take over the motorcycle stock of Mr. Lambert.

Lambert will remain at 33 East Franklin Street, and will continue in the bicycle sales and bicycle repair business and will also operate a Tire and Serivice Station.

Hagerstown Morning Herald October 1, 1925

Chester and Ray Delphey were the younger brothers of Frederick, Maryland H-D dealer J. Paul Delphey. Both younger men were World War I veterans who had received heralded welcomes home from the war. Chester, a grief-stricken teenaged widower, had enlisted after his wife's death as a motorcycle messenger. Once home he became an up-and-coming Class-A professional racer. Chester won the Maryland state championship in 1921 but is also responsible for the near banning of motorcycle racing in

38

Baltimore due to an incident that day that the papers termed "a riot." The race was at the old Prospect Park track, now occupied by Eastpoint Mall in east Baltimore.

Chester and sidecar rider Oscar Liddie had won the Baltimore race by a wide margin over another Class-A pro, Bill Minnick of Wilmington Delaware. But the pair from Frederick, were immediately disqualified. The Motorcycle and Allied Trades Association officials disapproved of Liddie's use of his body weight to assist Delphey in turning. Up until this time, it was normal for a racing sidecar passenger to tuck fully inside the bullet-shaped compartment for the whole race to reduce wind resistance. Chester and Oscar had discovered the advantages to be gained in the corners by the passenger instead leaning his weight onto and with the bike, then tucking back into the compartment on the straights.

While this tactic would become the universally employed and accepted practice for sidecar racing to the present, Oscar Liddie was doing something never before seen in July of 1921. Chester and Oscar, supported by a large contingent of fans who had thoroughly enjoyed Liddie's innovative performance stormed the official's stand to protest the men's disqualification. By news accounts, some of them demonstrated their displeasure by destroying some Prospect Park fixtures on the way.

According to the paper, it was only the intervention of several Maryland State Police motorcycle officers that saved the race officials from certain violence. The officials prudently decided to reverse their decision and restore Chester and Oscar's State Championship win.

It was a bittersweet victory. Later that same year tragedy struck in September, during a race in Winchester, Virginia. Liddie, using the same tactic would allow the sidecar to lift completely off the ground in the turns. During the last lap as it appeared they would add another win, as the sidecar slammed back onto the track at the end of turn two at full speed, …the axel broke.

Oscar and Chester were hurled down the back straight of the Winchester track in a violent high side crash obscured in a cloud of thick khaki dust. Amazingly, none of the following riders hit the unconscious victims as they lay on the track enshrouded by swirling dust. Wearing only the rudimentary safety gear of the period, the worst was feared by everyone present. Amazingly, both men recovered from the injuries but Chester suffered severe, lasting damage to both ankles that ended his promising racing career.

Ray Delphey, unlike his three brothers who all held jobs in the motorcycle industry, was a talented musician with a

successful entertainment career in Washington D.C. where he lived. It can be assumed Ray was a silent partner and perhaps a temporary investor as well. Chester is noted for years later as sole owner of the Hagerstown store.

Ned Lambert, as mentioned, would go on to several more "firsts" in Hagerstown. Family photos and news reports, however, still show evidence of an interest in motorcycles for many years afterward.

The Delphey dealership would occupy several venues around Hagerstown before moving to his lasting and remembered location on May 1, 1948. Delphey built a new store at 237 East Franklin Street just two blocks from the first shop. The new store though, did not include motorcycles. Chester, like his brother Paul in Frederick, would expand into boats and general sporting goods as well as being the local office for the Maryland Motor Vehicle Administration. In addition to being a successful businessman, Chester was also active in politics, serving as a county commissioner from 1950 until 1962 including his last term as president of the Board of Commissioners. Chester also served many years on the democratic central committee.

42

Chester's connections to other racers would continue to buoy his interest in motorcycle competition. For a time during the mid-century, he promoted amateur and even professional hill climb competitions near Kemp's Mill and later, Cearfoss, west of Hagerstown. As well, he continued to partner with his brothers, J. Paul and Clarence in promoting the annual July 4th race on the ½ mile track at the Frederick fairgrounds which J. Paul had begun in 1921.

To casual observers, Chester Delphey appears to have lived a carefree, cavalier life of success and prominence. He was successful. He was prominent. But Chester's life was one of unseen turmoil.

Hill Climbing Race Is Staged on Sunday

A large crowd was on hand for the hill climbing contests staged on Sunday at Kemp's Mill by the Hagerstown Motorcycle Club, with the following winners in the six events:

Hagerstown Club event, won by Clarence Feigley, Walter Stoddard second and Earl Hann third, time 6 2-5.

Open event, won by John Tanner, Baltimore; D. W. Hennis, Phillipsburg, Pa., second and Max Block, Baltimore, third. Time 5 2-5.

Amateur won by Bud Cosgrove, Cumberland, C. Frank, Harrisburg, Pa., second and Herman Cosgrove, Cumberland, third. Time 6.

Expert, D. H. Hennis, first, John Tanner second, Bert Cosgrove third. Time 5 1-5.

Expert, Bud Cosgrove first, D. W. Hennis second and Walter Stoddard third. Time 5 4-5.

The hill was 175 feet from starting line to top.

May 1929

Chester Delphey Has Raced Motorcycles, Shot Grizzly Bears; Loves Out-Of-Doors

By PHIL EBERSOLE

Chester F. Delphey, Chairman of the Washington County Democratic Central Committee, has loved adventure in the out-of-doors, from the time he was a teen-age motorcycle racer to the day in 1959 when he stalked and killed a 600-pound grizzly bear in the mountains of Wyoming.

"If I die tomorrow," Delphey said one day last week, "I haven't missed much".

The lobby of his business (now operated by his daughter) on W. Franklin St. reflects his love of life and the outdoors. Filled with rock samples, stationary, and the stuffed heads of elk, deer, moose and antelope killed by Delphey, it looks like the Wyoming branch of the Smithsonian Institution.

Motorcycle Racer

Delphey, who is 67, was born in Union Bridge, Md., and moved to Frederick with his parents and brothers as a boy of six. One of his brothers, J. Paul Delphey, started a used motorcycle business.

CHESTER DELPHEY

likes to drop in from time to time and look around, however.

Today the business is limited to the selling of automobile, hunting, fishing, and dog licen-

three wives by death, and Connie is his only child.

As a youth in Frederick, Delphey said, he registered as a Republican, like his brothers, when he came of age. Watching a nomination of a Republican candidate for mayor of Frederick by "a dirty deal", he said, he and his brothers walked out in disgust and registered Democratic. He has been a staunch Democrat ever since.

Delphey ran for public office three times, and was successful all three terms. He served two terms as County Commissioner, 1950-54, and 1954-58, and was elected chairman of the County Commissioners in 1955. In May, 1962, he and fellow members of the "white ticket" swept the incumbent Democratic central committee out of office, and Delphey was named chairman of the committee.

Important Job

One important job of the central committee is recommending appointees for pol-

1965 article about Delphey, then serving as chairman of the county Democratic central committee

Two of his closest friends lost their lives as successful young men in the sport all three shared a passion for. One in a boat accident, with Chester driving the boat. Chester's first wife died when she was only 18 a year after their marriage. His second wife died from an accident in their home at 32 while Chester was at work, leaving him to raise a young daughter. His third wife died in an auto collision in Virginia on a Christmas visit to her mother's house in 1948. Chester was again, at the wheel. Chester Delphey died in 1976 a lonely, seventy-eight years old. A prosperous, successful, and silently burdened man.

Washington county hill climbs about 1930

October 12, 1935 Advertisement for Delphey hill climb

J. Paul and Chester Delphey congratulating Harley-Davidson's legendary Joe Petrali at the 1935 Frederick, MD national championship race.

The three young musketeers. Photo of Bill Minnick with pet raccoon following his win at the 1925 Labor Day race on the Laurel Maryland board track riding a Delphey bike. The man beside him has been identified as his friend, sponsor, and sometimes racing rival, then 28-year-old Chester Delphey. The young man between them is thought to be (then 21-year-old) Walter Stoddard. Bill Minnick would lose his life in 1927 while leading a championship race near the Harley-Davidson factory in WI.

NEW MOTORCYCLE

Motor Patrolman John Knode has returned to Hagerstown with the new police motorcycle. He rode the new machine from the factory in Milwaukee, Wisconsin.

This 1930's photo does not appear to be John Knode, but neither does it seem to be the new 1934 VL model. While identity is uncertain, the other motorcycle patrolmen with HPD during the 1930's include Roy E. Davis, William Bloom, and Oscar C. Ambrose.

Gen II

While the 1930's are typically remembered for the desperation wrought by the great depression, the decade saw the maturing of those who embraced the invention of the motorcycle. The decade also ushered in the second generation of motorcycle enthusiasts.

The young men of the 30's had grown up with the popping roar of internal combustion engines and had never known a town without convenient, towering, gasoline pumps at every store and tavern. The bikes of the first decade with once *"powerful"* one or two horse-power engines, were already relegated to junk piles in the presence of machines producing many times that amount of power.

Motorcycle guys on Rt. 40 west 1930. Note race poster over door.

Early imported British bike riders

Most of the motorcycle business remained in the centrally convenient Hagerstown area and newspaper ads throughout the mid-century reflect the names of various dealers serving the motorcycle trade. Most of those businesses are no more than a curiosity today. Unrecognized names associated with now unknown business locations around the city no longer existing or recognizable. One of them though, would stand out. One of them proving himself up to challenging the test of time.

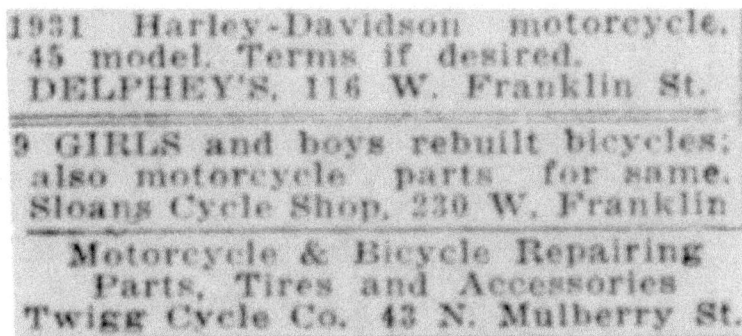

1931 Harley-Davidson motorcycle, 45 model. Terms if desired. DELPHEY'S, 116 W. Franklin St.

9 GIRLS and boys rebuilt bicycles; also motorcycle parts for same. Sloans Cycle Shop, 230 W. Franklin

Motorcycle & Bicycle Repairing Parts, Tires and Accessories Twigg Cycle Co. 43 N. Mulberry St.

The "Motorcycle & Bicycle" category of the Sept. 19, 1936, Morning Herald

Delphey's of course, we're familiar with from the previous chapter. 116 W. Franklin Street would be Delphey's short-lived second location.

Sloan's Cycle Shop, at 230 W. Franklin Street which would take over the H-D brand for a short time after Delphey gave it up, is today an empty lot. Twigg Cycle

Company though is a name still very familiar to Washington County motorcyclists.

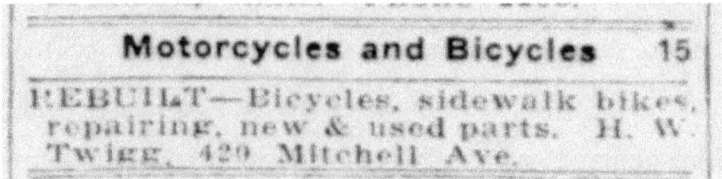

Dec. 1933 ad for H.W. Twigg bicycle shop on Mitchell Ave.

A faded 1937 ad for the popular 45 cubic inch (750cc) *"Sport Scout"* from Hagerstown's new Indian Motorcycle Company franchise. The name is familiar. The address, 43 N. Mulberry Street may be a surprise.

52

The first documented Indian in Hagerstown was John Rowland's 1905 model he traded a car to Murray Brish for in Frederick. John Connor and Ned Lambert announced their partnership selling Indians in 1910. Sam Haines sold them on W. Antietam for two years, then John Conner moved the dealership to S. Potomac Street until H. William Twigg moved it again in 1936 to N. Mulberry St., then Cannon Avenue. Grandson Mike Twigg restored the brand to Twigg's in 2012. Indians have been sold in Hagerstown from 1910 until the present – *if Indians were being made.*

According to family tradition, Mr. Twigg began his business as a young man in 1932, repairing bicycles around the neighborhood. He soon began selling parts and eventually new bicycles but still operated out of his mother's kitchen and the backdoor of the family home. Like most his age, his interest soon turned toward faster, more powerful machines and in 1936, he made the foreseeable next step from bicycles to motorcycles when he acquired Conner's Hagerstown Indian franchise.

Known affectionately for much of his life as *"Pappy,"* and often with a smirk by the speaker by his given name *"Horace,"* Bill Twigg would find lasting success with the Indian brand in Hagerstown. In the 1930's the State of Maryland began regulating motorcycle dealers. Bill dutifully bought his license as law required. Today, the business still holds the same license number M0002. The oldest continuously existing motorcycle dealer in the state of Maryland.

Financially, the Indian brand never fully recovered from World War II. The only post-war Indian model made was the top of the line, Chief and even production of new Chief's ceased in 1949. Some assembly from inventory continued into 1950 and following acquisition by a British firm, imported (Royal Enfield) motorcycles were re-branded and sold under the Indian name for a short time, but the end of an era had come.

The full story is much more complicated. As Indian historian R. L. Lyons explained, it includes fallout from political maneuvering dating to the mid-30's before the war even began and parties to it remaining in office long afterward. Part of that story involves the post-war opening given to imported motorcycles for the first time and the detrimental effect that would have for both American brands. Harley-Davidson appealed to the U.S. Congress in 1950 claiming unfair practices by foreign makers. Domestic production *decreased* from 27,400 to 20,600 between 1949 and 1950 due mostly to Indian's slump while imports skyrocketed from 5,342 in 1949 to 10,192 in 1950. Congress refused to intervene and the domestic industry was left to fight for its own survival.

Luckily for H. William Twigg, he had already diversified his business by adding several other brands to the Twigg tent. By embracing the daggers which the government allowed to be thrown at domestic motorcycle production, Bill Twigg was able to salvage his own business by turning the development to his advantage.

Riding a CZ "125" is effortless!

Only the CZ has ALL of these 8 valuable features:

✓ APPEARANCE   ✓ PICK-UP
✓ WORKMANSHIP   ✓ SPEED
✓ LOW PRICE   ✓ COMFORT
✓ ECONOMY   ✓ SAFETY

Another outstanding motorcycle of the JAWA Family!
Come in for a demonstration.

TWIGG CYCLE CO.
38 N. Cannon Avenue
Hagerstown, Md.

Aug. 5, 1949 (Czechoslovakian) **CZ Motorcycles ad**

Being one of the first to embrace the then new imported lightweight cycles entering the U.S. market may have been viewed as questionable by the established riders of big, fully dressed Indians and Harleys that made up the core of the 1940's American motorcycle market, but Bill Twigg couldn't have made a better decision if he'd had a crystal ball to tell the future.

55

Home from the war, 40's era riders. Some still in uniform.

While many today still consider the British brands as *the* competition to Indian and Harley in the 1950's, Czechoslovakia was a close second regarding U.S. motorcycle imports during this entry period for non-domestic bikes. The now little known, Czechoslovakian CZ's would be the first, but Twigg added other imports to his new showroom on Cannon Avenue. Ideally locating that new shop between the lanes of the Dual Highway, which was then and for decades afterward often crowded with cruising teenagers and young adults. The shop was across the street from Delphey's back lot, where everyone in the county got their driver's license. It was a move that showed more of H. William Twigg's business sense.

For many years Twigg's Cycles provided a courtesy to those who asked by allowing the borrow of a lightweight "shop bike" to take the motorcycle proficiency test in the lot behind Delphey's. It meant a learner didn't have to arrange for someone else, a licensed rider, to take off work and accompany them for the test. For some, it meant they didn't have to negotiate the obstacle course on the less nimble, big heavy machines they had at home. Even some who didn't yet own a motorcycle would obtain their license thanks to Twigg's generosity. Ultimately, before the Motor Vehicle Administration moved to their new location in the 1980's, countless local motorcyclists would remember that they obtained their license thanks to the benevolence of Pap Twigg.   And when they wanted service, parts, or a new motorcycle, many of them remembered that courtesy.

The 1950's into the 1960's saw a marked change in the American motorcycle market. Racing, that constant driver of motorcycle development and interest since its introduction, had found new outlets other than the big, power-dependent, track racing that had been its mainstay since the beginning. Most of the new motorcycle sports were "off-road" activities. Sports that *demanded* the use of agile, lightweight bikes. This new direction culminated in the explosion of interest in motocross in the 1970's.

57

Simultaneous to this redirection, in truth, the driver of it, was the emergence of the baby boom generation.

Millions of young people, the ones most likely to take up motorcycling, poured into the motorcycle market and they wholeheartedly embraced these new imported brands. Pap Twigg welcomed them to the fold with open arms …and a big new showroom full of CZ's, Parilla's, Ariels, BMW's, Triumphs, BSA's …and ultimately, Yamahas.

1957 BSA ad

Twigg's Cycles, while the longest lasting dealer, not only in Washington County but in Maryland, was not the only success story during this magical motorcycle era spanning the 1960's through the early 2000's. Twigg's 1998 move to the present location at 200 Edgewood Drive as Hagerstown itself spread outward, was just another step along the path Pap Twigg started down in 1932. But there is one more chapter to Pap Twigg's story before moving on to other local motorcycle businesses.

The *Indian Motorcycles* name has carried an almost mystic aura since the company's untimely demise in 1950. Since then, several companies sought to revive the brand and capitalize on the nostalgia of what had been the premiere, classic American motorcycle. The result is a long list of failed *former* Indian motorcycle companies.

Finally, the successful inventor of the snowmobile, *Polaris Incorporated*, purchased the company name and intellectual property in 2011. Today built in Spirit Lake Iowa, Polaris, with their proven track record in the powersports industry, has triumphantly succeeded where others had failed in restoring the once proud Indian brand. On the road *and* on the track.

As a then existing Polaris dealer, Twigg's immediately leaped on the opportunity to restore Pap Twigg's original line of motorcycles to their other offerings. Today, Twigg's Cycles contests as one of the largest volume Indian motorcycle dealers anywhere. They are *definitely* one of the oldest. Still carrying the torch for a 117-year Hagerstown tradition.

**Installing the Indian sign in front of the new Cannon Av. shop.
Bill Twigg 2nd from top.** (Courtesy of Andy DeLauder)

61

Throughout the twentieth century there have been many new motorcycle dealers in and around Hagerstown. All but two have come and gone with various degrees of individual longevity. Chester Delphey's sporting goods business and the ever-increasing space required by the motor vehicle administration offices prompted the sale of his Harley-Davidson dealership. It passed through various hands at many different locations around the city for decades. The last was Paul Kitchen and Roy Bower's shop across the street from Twiggs. One 1966 newspaper article referred to the first block of N. Cannon Avenue as "*motorcycle alley.*" The shop closed about 1970, but in 2003, Mike Vantucci, the owner of the Frederick Maryland Harley-Davidson franchise opened "**Harley-Davidson of Williamsport**" in that neighboring town. Twenty-five years earlier, Mike had bought the Frederick business from "Delphey's Sport Shop," originally *J. Paul Delphey's Harley-Davidson*. Paul was of course, Hagerstown Harley dealer Chester Delphey's older brother.

The author's 1920's era forged steel Delphey screwdriver.

There would of course be other brands sold by various dealers. As well, there have been many shops right up to the present dealing solely in used bikes, independent, service, restoration, aftermarket parts and or repair without offering new bikes for sale. A few unexpected outlets even tried to capitalize on the popularity of motorcycling in the 1960's and 70's.

65

On June 23, 1971, a new ad appeared under the *"Motorcycles and Bicycles"* category of the Daily Mail classifieds section. It promised something exciting.

HONDA
OF
HAGERSTOWN

Re-invents the motorcycle dealership - starting this Saturday.

THEN, see the area's only

CB500 - 4

HONDA of HAGERSTOWN
Rte. 40 & I-70
Phone 301-797-7200

June 26, 1971 would be the grand opening of Hagerstown's newest motorcycle dealership and the local arrival of the Honda marque. Among the various Japanese brands which had entered the American market during the nineteen-sixties, by 1971, Honda was well on its way to being #1. In 1970 though, Washington countians still had to go to Chambersburg, Frederick, or more distant cities to buy a new Honda.

Honda motorcycles were immensely popular in 1970. In the lightweight (under 500cc) category which the Japanese had specifically targeted when moving into the American market, Honda held the greatest share.

In 1960 the 125cc Harley-Davidson "Hummer," was all the American company offered below the big 900cc and larger, full-sized bikes Harley was famous for. The Japanese, led by Honda and Yamaha, pounced on what they rightly perceived as a huge, underserved market share. Harley management, realizing they had made a mistake by ignoring the lightweight segment for so long, quickly sought to plug the gap in what they considered their personal and deserved market.

Harley-Davidson's solution, in part driven by the need to act quickly, was deciding that it was more prudent to buy an already producing light-weight motorcycle company than to endure the multi-year process of creating and testing their own new designs from the ground up and tooling up a new factory to produce them. The result was the 1960 purchase of a controlling share of the Italian Aeromacchi factory.

Eventually, Harley engineers and American tastes would contribute to design innovations, but during the 100, 125, 250 and 350cc bike's eighteen-year inclusion as Italian built but Harley-Davidson branded motorcycles, they never saw the widespread acceptance the Japanese imports did. They were quality little bikes but were never accepted as either "true Harleys" by established, Harley-Davidson customers *or* as competitive with the Japanese imports by new, entry level customers.

By 1979 Harley sold their interest in the Italian company and concentrated on domestic production of big bikes. They conceded the lightweight category as they were now struggling even to maintain their heavy-weight market share against innovative modern designs as the Japanese advanced into that segment as well.

It was a perfect wave. There continued to be millions of young baby boomers pouring into the motorcycle market every year. It was an unprecedented period of economic prosperity. Combined with the ready availability of modern, reliable, technologically advanced, *and inexpensive* bikes, it resulted in a boom of historic proportion for the Japanese manufacturers.

Many of the lightweights from both Japan and Europe were two-strokes. Originally and for many years afterward, many two-stroke engines required mixing a specifically measured amount of special oil with the gasoline whenever the fuel tank was filled.

Honda, from their entry into the U.S. market was an exception in that most of their motorcycles used four-stroke engines like American bikes. This meant that the gas tank could be filled directly from the pump. This carefree element for even the smallest minibikes simplified life for entry-level enthusiasts and made Honda even more inviting and popular. As a final measure in attracting riders who might not otherwise entertain motorcycling, Honda adopted an enormous national marketing campaign promoting the catchy phrase *"You meet the nicest people on a Honda."* With a convenient location then far out on the dual highway among farms and fields, and with a specious lot surrounding the big building, Don Meyers' Honda of Hagerstown, definitely promoted the more civil side of motorcycling.

The local paper's 1972 Christmas advertising campaign included appearances at participating businesses by *"Merri Christmas."* Mr. Meyers apparently thought it'd help sell Christmas minibikes.

Then, in October 1973 the Arab oil embargo, for the first time since the internal combustion engine was invented, made gasoline both scarce and uncommonly expensive – for the period. Prices quickly surpassed the unheard-of level of fifty cents per gallon. There were wild rumors it would go as high as $1.00!

Americans, used to long solo commutes, and typically in large, gas guzzling cars, were suddenly faced with unexpected costs and even an unprecedented uncertainty of even reaching their destinations in some cases. Huge fuel storage tanks ran dry and gas stations closed. Governments restricted allowed re-fueling days and a new, prior to now unfamiliar term, *"miles-per-gallon"* entered the American vocabulary.

In December 1973, instead of "Merri Christmas," Don Meyers' Honda of Hagerstown took out an expensive full-page ad extolling the advantages of riding a Honda as everyday transportation. It was reasoning difficult to argue with. On an economical motorcycle, you could travel to work all week on as much gas as your two-ton Plymouth used in one day for the same commute. It was reasoning that brought even more unlikely riders into the motorcycle market. An acquaintance recently related how he and his girlfriend rode his Honda from Hagerstown to College Park every day, while attending college in the 1970's.

The motorcycle as

alternate transportation.

THE FUEL SHORTAGE

There's a lot of talk about the fuel shortage. Gas rationing. Gas costing one dollar per gallon. 50 m.p.h. speed limits. And all the rest.

The Environmental Protection Agency, in mileage testing of 1973 cars, came up with some figures that are awesome, in relation to the possibility of high-cost gasoline.

As an example, one medium-priced, medium-sized American car, with automatic transmission and an engine of about 350 cubic inches, was tested and got 9.5 miles to the gallon of gas.

FUEL COST & THE CAR

To use round figures (and some speculation): A round trip from Hagerstown to Chambersburg is about 50 miles. If your automobile is getting 10 miles per gallon, and gas goes to $1.00 per gallon, it would cost you $5.00 to make that trip.

Five dollars. If you make the trip five days a week, that is twenty-five dollars a week for gas alone. Right now, you're probably spending about twelve dollars per week for that trip. And watching the cost slowly creep up.

OTHER TRANSPORTATION

There are alternatives. Get a smaller car. Join, or form, a car pool. Use public transportation.

Or, get a motorcycle.

There are a number of advantages, and disadvantages, in a motorcycle as transportation. Let's look at the disadvantages first.

MOTORCYCLE DISADVANTAGES

In bad weather, a motorcycle can be a bad trip. Particularly when it's raining, or snowing, or precipitating some other way. And, when it's cold, you're gonna be cold, UNLESS you go prepared. A fairing (optional) offers a fair amount of protection, but proper clothing is the best protection.

A motorcycle is another motor vehicle, re-

quiring a license and insurance. And, it requires taking another operator's test.

Now, if we haven't scared you off, we'll discuss the advantages.

MOTORCYCLE ADVANTAGES

With a street motorcycle, like our CB450, you can get over 40 miles to that gallon of gas. That's traveling at highway speeds. Being smaller, it's more maneuverable than an automobile. And, there's parking - a dream. Maintenance costs are cheaper. Also, unlike public transportation, or car pools, you can go where you want, when you want.

Actually, we think one of the greatest things about a motorcycle is an intangible. It's a feeling of freedom. In this regimented, over-conforming society in which we live, a motorcycle is capable of giving you that feeling that you're in control of what you're doing and where you're going. You and the bike and the road and the wind. Watergate, the Middle East, shortages, life's problems, they all seem so far away. Ride and enjoy. At one-eighth the fuel cost of that medium-sized car. Who says you can't have your cake and eat it, too?

WHY A HONDA?

It's very simple. Honda sells more motorcycles in the U.S. than any other company. We have 32 different models. More dealers than any other make. And we sell quality. Motorcycles that are well-built, and reliable. Honda has it all.

ANY QUESTIONS?

We've tried to lightly touch on the subject of motorcycles as transportation. If you have any other questions, any at all, please feel free to ask us. We're open till 8 Tuesday through Friday, and till 5 on Saturday. And we like to talk about motorcycles almost as much as we like riding them.

Honda of Hagerstown

Rte. 40 & I-70   797-7200

More than fifty-years after being firmly relegated to the recreational vehicle category, motorcycles were once more being suggested, *and seriously considered* by many, as a genuine everyday transportation alternative.

When photos of John Wayne on the set of "The Cowboys" showed him on a SL350 Honda, could the American acceptance of the brand be any more complete?

Another major Japanese brand, which already had a devoted local following, finally found a home at 640 Frederick Street in Hagerstown during the summer of 1976. **Hagerstown Kawasaki** would be a familiar fixture on Frederick Street for several years while the brand won countless races on the Motocross tracks, drag strips, and more than a few public roads.

Kawasaki Was a late entry into the motorcycle industry. They only entered the field in 1964 when they took over Japan's (once) largest and oldest maker, Meguro Motorcycles. Kawasaki's industrial presence, and its dominance in numerous industries, dates to Shozo Kawasaki's efforts in the shipbuilding business in the 1890's. Before expanding into motorcycles, Kawasaki had mastered shipbuilding, locomotives, automobiles, airplanes, and helicopters! They invested in the struggling Meguro in 1960 and took over full control four years later. Like everything they had done previously, when Kawasaki began building their own motorcycles, their goal was to build the best. It would take some brand building to ramp up to a position of international contention but while the bar was high, Kawasaki was an experienced jumper.

Motorcycle brand loyalty can be a touchy subject. You won't find me picking any favorites between these covers but in 2014, at the last national championship race completed at Hagerstown Speedway, the first time a brand *other than* Harley-Davidson won the Hub City Classic, or a ½ mile race anywhere in 20-years, it was Bryan Smith, - on a Kawasaki.

As the various dealerships went away over the years, Twigg's acquired the orphaned franchises together with several other marquees of various powersports equipment.

The tradition begun by Pappy Twigg more than 85 years-ago, continues today under the direction of grandson Mike Twigg and great-grandchildren Brock and Stephanie. Home to six different brands, except for the previously mentioned Williamsport Harley-Davidson shop, Twigg's is the only other *new* motorcycle dealership in Washington County today.

There continue as well to be various independent shops practicing service, restoration, and modification services around the county. As the baby boom generation ages and economic conditions ebb and flow. Even as the availability of opportunities for interested youngsters to ride changes, the motorcycle business boom of the second half of the last century continues to change as well. Where it will lead in the next 130-years remains an unanswered question, but we have a rich past to build on.

RACING

No book on motorcycles is complete without a discussion of racing. Regarding motorcycle history, there may be none to discuss if it wasn't for racing in the earliest days of the motorcycle. Racing runs through everything motorcycle related

Entrance sign, Antietam Motosport Park, Hagerstown

In the first chapter we touched on the earliest racing dating to 1900 in conjunction with the *"League of American Wheelmen."* Races that were more curiosity than competition when motorcycles were essentially a category of bicycles. At the time, when horses were still the only means of vehicle propulsion, the mere sight of those early motorcycles reaching the insane speeds of 30-40mph was amazing.

In 1903, designer Glenn Curtiss set the world speed record [motorcycle category] of 64mph in Younkers N.Y. Just four years later, Curtiss would more than double his old record at Ormond Beach FL. In 1912 a popular period attraction visited Hagerstown. A motorcycle racing against a biplane around the fairground track! Amazingly to us today, the motorcycle was the easy winner. The plane typically only reaching about 40-45 mph.

Then too, until World War II, essentially all entertainment required spectators to attend events. Whether races or ballgames, the only alternative to seeing it in person was reading about it the next day in the newspaper. Such events would regularly draw crowds of thousands, even in cities like Hagerstown. Special trollies would be run to the fairgrounds. Even special trains from outside the city were scheduled to address the influx of fans. In the larger metropolitan areas, professional motorcycle racing was for a time in the first decades of the century, the #2 spectator sport in the nation. Closely challenging baseball for #1.

On Decoration Day May 30, 1911, when Hagerstown's population was 16,507, the fairgrounds races drew over

5,000 ticket buying spectators. The morning Herald told the story the following day.

Motorcycle Race.

The motorcycle race was one of the most pleasing features of the day. There were five entries in this race. J. R. Miller, of Philadelphia, who rode an Indian motorcycle gave some feats of fast riding, making the mile in 1 minute. The winners in the motorcycle race follow:

John Rowland, first; Ralph Frushour, second and Clarence Henneberger, third. The time was 6 minutes 29½ seconds.

Readers may recall that race winner John Rowland, bought his first (documented) motorcycle in 1905 when he traded in a car as part of the deal with Murray Brish in Frederick. All entrants except J.R. Miller were local men. We can assume this was a local, amateur race. Assumedly, Miller, obviously an experienced racer, was brought in by [1910] Hagerstown Indian dealers Ned Lambert and John Conner to showcase their product. That was then a common business practice. Oddly, neither Conner, nor Lambert are listed as entries. Perhaps to avoid alienating potential customers. Conner and his brother Tom were well-known, and popular riders who would have a notable, though brief, professional racing career. Apparently, since he's not listed in the results, Miller was just giving an exhibition.

As seen previously, the original motorcycle races in Hagerstown were held in conjunction with the bicycle racing events that were so popular around the turn of the 20th century.   Later races would be features of other sporting events before the discipline reached the point of sustaining events on its own. Until after WW-II, all track racing was on the old fairgrounds track.

By 1910, motorcycle racing became a mainstay of the regularly scheduled events held by the *"driving clubs,"* around the region. These organizations were the sponsors of Harness racing, which was arguably the most popular form of horse racing during the period. These race meets would draw thousands of spectators yet news reports from the teens and twenties from Hagerstown to Salisbury mention the included motorcycle events as the most pleasing, exciting, or entertaining of all the features of the day.

Professional

MOTORCYCLE
HILL CLIMB

Direction

Hagerstown Motorcycle Club

SUNDAY

MAY 5th — 1:30 P. M.
Hill At Kemp's Mill
4 Miles West of City

4 BIG EVENTS 4

Professional Riders
Hot Competition
SANCTIONED HILL CLIMB

Hag. Morning Herald, May 2, 1929

PETRALI RETAINS

HIS HILL CLIMB TITLE

Record crowd Turns Out

For Interesting Motor-

Cycle Events

Joe Petrali and "Buck" Rieber split

honors in the class A events of the

motorcycle hill climb held yesterday

afternoon on one of the stiffest climbs

in these parts, located six miles west of

Hagerstown along Cearfoss Pike.   A

Crowd of some 2,500 fans witnessed the

Events which were run off without a hitch.

Petrali was the first in the class A event

And second in the other event in the class

A event in a class A competition. Rieber

second and a first in the same clas ᵀ

class B event, Cosgrove ᵒᶠ

ᶠⁱʳˢᵗ and

Partial clipping from 1936 AMA Class A Pro Hill Climb

Joe Petrali was a star H-D factory rider and multiple discipline national champion. His world record of 136.183 mph, set on the beach at Daytona lasted 11 years. That year, at the peak of his career in 1937, at 33 years old, Petrali retired from pro racing. In truth, he had been personally recruited by an admiring fan to help perfect   his aircraft engines. The fan's name was Howard Hughes.

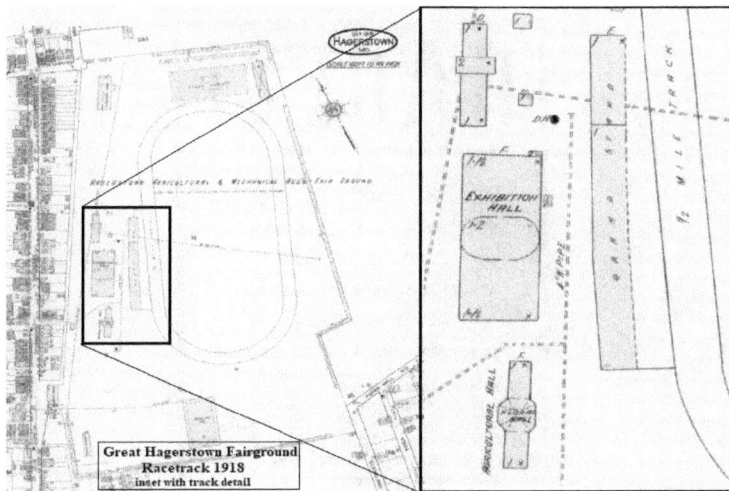

Great Hagerstown Fairground
Racetrack 1918
inset with track detail

An excerpt from the 1918 Sanborn maps of Hagerstown indicating the location and length of the old fairgrounds track. The very long straights and perfectly radiused turns in a paperclip layout gave the track the appearance of being much larger. Most who remember it, are surprised that it was only ½ mile. The grandstands positioned much higher than the racing surface gave great views of the entire track. The generous width is obvious in this illustration by comparison to the still existing grandstand building. Racetrack length is *officially* measured 18" from the inside edge, thus explaining the deceptive appearance of being larger. What an awesome track it must have been for motorcycles. *Wide open all the way around!* The track is gone today, and the property has been converted to other uses by the new owner, …the city of Hagerstown.

RACES!

SEE THE SPEED DEMONS

Saturday, June 18, 2 p. m.

AT THE HAGERSTOWN
FAIR GROUNDS

3—Hours Real Thrills—3

6—Exciting Races—6

Most dare-devil of all racing

5 Mile Motorcycle
10 Mile Side-car professional
15 Mile Side-car championship
5 Mile automobile, lady drivers
10 and 25 Mile auto, open professional races.

$1,800.00 IN PRIZES
Biggest Ever In Maryland

ADMISSION, 50c and $1.00
Including grandstand & war tax
TICKETS ON SALE AT
Hamilton Cigar Stand
Rudy's Cigar Store
Wash. and Jonathan Sts.
Lambert's Motorcycle Shop
33 E. Franklin St.

Daily Mail, June 17, 1921

Shadow of Hagerstown
Fairground Track 1998

86

GRAND GALA HOLIDAY

FAIRGROUNDS, Hagerstown, Md.,

Thursday, Decoration Day, MAY 30

Hagerstown Driving Club's

ANNUAL EVENT.   BIGGER AND BETTER THAN EVER

SENSATIONAL AEROPLANE FLIGHTS AND RACES

EXCITING HORSE RACES

"CLASSY" HORSE SHOW.

BICYCLE AND MOTORCYCLE RACES.

MUSIC—BANDS GALORE—MUSIC

GREAT PARADE IN THE MORNING.

EXCURSION RATES ON ALL RAILROADS.

Admission--25c--Admission

May 18, 1912, ad for Fairgrounds Decoration Day events

Lovers of motorcycle races who cannot get a first-hand thrill out of watching a cluster of hooded speed demons whirling around a race track on fire-spitting, two-wheeled devils are in for some rare entertainment at the Fairgrounds on Saturday, September 30.

So began the colorful September 20 article announcing the big races in Hagerstown two Saturdays later. The median annual income in the U.S. in 1920 was $1,407. The motorcycle races scheduled for the Hagerstown fairgrounds on Sept. 30, 1922, advertised a cash purse of $600. Admission was seventy-five cents and later reports would put the crowd at over 5,000 ticket buying spectators. There was much more at stake than mere entertainment.

One of the most successful of many motorcycle racers to come out of Hagerstown was Walter Stoddard, to whom this book is dedicated.

Walter Stoddard 1930

Walter Stoddard was from the rural community of Reid between Hagerstown Maryland and Waynesboro, Pennsylvania. Walt's Dad, Eugene Stoddard was the constable for the Reid area. It is unknown how motorcycles became integrated into the family, but the machines were obviously well incorporated to the Stoddard household by at least 1918 when the earliest mention is found in a story regarding Walter's older brother Howard having his leg broken in two places. Howard didn't crash, he was kicked by a horse that obviously did not like the noisy machine. Walt began his career in the motorcycle industry as a teenager working as a mechanic for Chester Delphey in Hagerstown soon after Delphey entered business here. Exhibiting great talent as a rider, he soon moved to

Frederick and technically went to work in Chester's brother, J. Paul Delphey's Harley shop there. In truth, Stoddard became the primary rider of the pro race team sponsored by Paul Delphey.

After Chester Delphey's career ending crash at Winchester Virginia in 1921, J. Paul had backed the efforts of Chester's friend and rival Bill Minnick for the following seven years. Then, on August 25, 1928, while leading a championship race at Carrollville Wisconsin, 10-miles from the Harley-Davidson factory, Bill Minnick, riding a Delphey bike, crashed through a wooden fence at close to 100mph. His injuries were fatal. It was these questionable circumstances that provided the opportunity for Walt Stoddard to become a professional racer, but in racing circles, opportunity is where, not how you find it.

In 1928 Walt received his Class-A racer's license from the American Motorcycle Association. AMA has been the sanctioning body of professional motorcycle racing from 1924 to the present.

Stoddard made a great showing for the Delphey team throughout 1928 and 1929. By mid-season of the second year, he had shown so much promise that opportunity came his way again. Walt Stoddard was offered a coveted ride on the Harley-Davidson factory racing team. In just three years, he had reached the pinnacle of the sport from humble beginnings in the tiny community of Reid Maryland.

Walter F. Stoddard had firmly arrived among the best of the best in the world. At only 26 years-old, his future looked very bright. Unfortunately for young Walt Stoddard, the bad luck which seemed to follow Delphey's racers was about to strike again. For Walt it would not be a racing incident.

On Thursday evening, July 2, 1931, while out for a motorboat ride with his friends, Chester Delphey, and Pete Everly near today's Big Slack Water boat ramp, the trio encountered engine trouble. Stoddard, as the expert mechanic, was leaning over the transom of the boat adjusting the motor when it suddenly lurched at full turn and capsized. The other two men swam to safety. Walt, having grown up at Reid where the only water over knee-deep on Marsh Run was in the Wingerton mill pond, couldn't swim and quickly drowned in the river.

Walter Stoddard, of this city, riding in the motorcycle races at the New York State fair, established a world's record in the 10 mile event when he won in the time of 7:23.06. Stoddard, whose home is in this city, finished third in the national championship five mile event which was won by Jim Davis, of Columbus, Ohio.

91

LOCAL RACER GETS TWO FIRST PLACES

Wins Three Races At Championship In Toronto

Walter Stoddard, local motorcycle racer and ace of this section, won two races at the Canadian National Championship events on Monday, held at Toronto, Canada.

The local boy, who was entered in the professional class, could only compete in three races. He placed second in the third race.

Stoddard, although robbed of $65 on a Pennsylvania tr 'n on his way to the races, between Hagerstown and New York, did not get discouraged and carried out his purpose of showing what he could do.

Stoddard, who has been in training for some time, will also compete in the big races at Richmond, Va., on Memorial Day, May 30. He is a mechanic for Delphy Bros., this city, and used a Harley-Davidson cycle in the races.

Hagerstown Morning Herald, May 27, 1930

Morning Herald, July 21, 1930

Walt's 50 sec. time on the original one-mile Arora Downs in 1930 is barely 10 sec. off the best time in "*The OKC Mile*" in 2021.

Walter Stoddard monument, Rose Hill cemetery, Hagerstown,

MAN DROWNS AS

BOAT OVERTURNS

ON THE POTOMAC

Walter Stoddard, 26 Loses

His Life Near Dam

No.4

TWO OTHERS ESCAPE

SWIMMING TO SHORE

Motorboat Capsizes After

Sharp Turn in

Deep Water

This story is even darker and much sadder than the preceding suggests. As is often the case, this tragedy changed numerous other's lives forever. Walt's grief-stricken little sister, 16-year-old Elsie, unexplainably died at his graveside the day of the funeral. Her official cause of death was heart failure. Making it all real for me was the discovery that Walter Stoddard's brother Howard, was the husband of my grandfather's own little sister Iola.

Despite this tragedy, interest in racing would continue unabated. Races continued being held at the fairgrounds and hill climbs continued at Cearfoss. But there were gathering clouds on the horizon.

In June 1942, J. Paul Delphey sent a letter to AMA headquarters in Columbus Ohio returning his sanction for the big July fourth race in Frederick and asking AMA president E.C. Smith, that AMA heed requests by President Roosevelt and Maryland governor O'Conner to halt *all* racing until after WW-II. A week later the AMA issued a notice suspending racing nationwide. Smith's announcement used some of the same language as Delphey's letter to him the previous week. Sanctioned motorcycle racing would not resume until 1947. By the time racing returned, there would be a new track in Washington County.

In 1946 businessman Stanley Schetromph began building a ½ mile red clay surfaced racetrack on the 52-acre site of Conococheague Amusement Park where Conococheague Creek is crossed by U.S. Route 40. Then, years before Inter-state 70, Rt. 40 was the main east-west highway. Schetromph originally named the track Conococheague Speedway. [*"Con-nuh-ka-jig"*]

Early Conococheague Speedway track crew

UNDER THE LIGHTS · 9 EVENTS - TIME TRIALS 7:30 P.M.

CONOCOCHEAGUE SPEEDWAY

6 Miles West of Hagerstown, Md. on Route 40

General Admission	$1.00
Bleachers - - -	1.25
Any Seat in Grandstand	1.75
ALL TAXES INCLUDED	

A M A   Class "C" 4 - STAR   A M A

PROFESSIONAL MOTORCYCLE RACES

FRI. NITE, JULY 22

Sponsored by: HAGERSTOWN MOTORCYCLE CLUB

July 22, 1949, Hagerstown national ad

Prior to the war, most motorcycle racing was staged on what had originally been horse tracks. In some locations,

97

it still is today. The horse track origins of the sport is where the popular name *"flat track"* comes from.

Conococheague Speedway was something brand new, not only its construction, but its very design. The track was built specifically for motor racing. The straight-a-ways are a *fast* 900 feet long and a generous 70 feet wide. Particularly unusual for older tracks are the corners. The turns at Conococheague, instead of tightening down like many horse tracks, are a welcomed 90 feet wide. 20 feet wider than the straights. To aid further in keeping speed up, the turns at Conococheague were given banking. The surface is a normally tacky red clay. Before this time, most sporting events were held during daylight hours. It was the only option. Conococheague though, featured new flood lighting that allowed the previously unheard-of option of night racing from its very beginning.

The track finally opened in 1948 and while the speedway was designed for cars, motorcycles were included in the annual schedule almost immediately.

After the close of the 1949 season, the name of the speedway was changed to *"**Hagerstown Speedway**."* AMA sanctioned motorcycle racing, featuring nationally ranked riders had been a staple at the speedway since its beginnings. Originally holding "regional" races that attracted riders seeking to make a paycheck between national circuit events, races were scheduled to compliment the travel plans of touring race teams. The track was however a featured and much anticipated stop on the AMA's Grand National Championship circuit at least twenty-seven times. One or more (GNC) National had been held in 1964, 1983, and annually from 1987-2015. Several years saw two nationals held in Hagerstown during the same season.

In July 2017, a start-up (non-GNC) series – The Steel Shoe National - held its inaugural race at the Hagerstown track with packed stands. The event drew many top ranked riders curious about the new series, but the parent organization fell apart after several races on western tracks and ceased to exist. At this writing, a motorcycle race has not been held at Hagerstown Speedway since 2017, but many motorcycle racers and race fans still hold hope for its return.

HAGERSTOWN
SPEEDWAY
BUD MESSNER
Presents

MOTORCYCLE
RACES

ADMISSION
Granstand $1.50
Bleachers 90c

RACING STARTS 2 P.M. DST
Sanctioned by A.M.A.
Motorcycle Association
★ 4 STAR EVENT
Top Riders and Plenty
of 'Em
Class A and Class B
Motorcycle Racing

Oct. 19, 1957

100

Motorcycles, including annual national championship races, were a regular part of the Hagerstown Speedway program until the track closed in 1964. When the track reopened under new management, it was a consortium of four motorcycle enthusiasts who reopened it *specifically for motorcycle races*. Only one of the new owners had ever seen a car race! Auto racing though, was eventually restored to the regular program in 1967 to help increase track profits.

Despite no AMA racing since 2015, countless former and current racers still call Hagerstown Speedway their favorite track in the country. Hagerstown Speedway was not however, the only track in the area.

1964 GNC champion, Dick Mann

1964 pre-race rider's meeting for the 50-lap race

Ted Heil, from Dayton OH. In 1964 at Hagerstown

Bob Sholly, from York, PA

Ohio rider, Ronnie Rall, 50-lap Hagerstown race 1965

Don Twigg #31, Billy Lloyd #64, Darryl Dovel #45, Gary Nixon #9

Hagerstown, 1965

Willie Moye, Philadelphia, PA. in 1965 at Hagerstown

Triumph (brand) riding Moye was one of the earliest African American professional racers to *officially* compete in AMA national competition. As in all professional sports before the 1960's, there was a separate, Negro Racing League with its own stars such as former NRL National Champion, Milton Hall. There are however many stories of men of either race competing covertly in the other's events *with the aid of official participants*. Racers just wanted to see who was the fastest. And Willie was *fast!* Sadly, Willie Moye lost his life in a crash at Heidelberg PA. the week after this photo was taken at Hagerstown.

A 1950's day at the races

Grandstand crowd for 1964 Hagerstown motorcycle races

#4 Bart Markel and #94 George Roeder, in 1964 at Hagerstown

Racing Here Tomorrow

Claude Dawson, above, of Waco, Texas, will be among the nation's leading motorcycle riders who will compete for cash and glory in the Four-Star cycle races at Hagerstown Speedway tomorrow afternoon. The popular Dawson won the eighth-mile National Dirt Track Championship at Shreveport, La., in October of last year.

Cycle Races Feature
July 4th Sports Card

There'll be plenty of fireworks at the Hagerstown Speedway tomorrow afternoon when over 100 of the nation's top motorcycle drivers compete for top honors in the four-star motorcycle meet.

Ad for 1950 Hagerstown race

Charles *"Charlie"* Miller #176c, Hagerstown (looking at camera)
Sponsored by Twigg's Indian Motorcycles, 1949 Frederick ½ mile

Live sports venues are in a transition period. Little more than two generations ago, seeing sports live, as it happened, could only happen by going to the event in-person to witness it. Television changed that. As the entertainment medium has evolved and eventually branched into the internet age, attending any sporting event has gradually become more about the event – the gathering itself – than it is the activity that takes place to host the event.

Of course, sports events have always been social affairs. They have always been commercial events. As the entertainment industry evolves in the 21st century, only time can tell where motorcycle racing will fall among the resulting chips. There is no comparison though between watching an event on TV or online and being there in person.

A televised event is restricted to what the camera is focused on at any given time and there is always much more going on around a racetrack! Frequently, the best race on the track is for 10th place. Racers want to race and none of them want to be last. The idea that there is only one winner and everyone else lost, doesn't apply if you are not the first-place rider. As the sport moves more and more toward broadcast, I hope some way can be found to assure live racing can continue or quite simply racing will not.

The photo on the cover of this book is from Little Heiskell motorcycle club's old track near Cearfoss. It is a shot of that year's Grand National Champion (1968) Gary Nixon riding an unidentified single cylinder motorcycle. Several nationally ranked pro racers appear in the photo below including novice class #29 Earl Myers of Hyattsville and Hagerstown's own expert class #31, Don Twigg.

An old photo from Little Heiskell MC Club

Nation's Top Riders To Compete Here On Sunday

Marvin Twigg, Paul Kiethen To Represent Hagerstown In Cycle Events; Over 100 Entries Are Expected

Motorcycle races will highlight the July 4th weekend action at the Hagerstown Speedway, featuring the annual appearance in this area of many of the nation's leading cyclists.

An action-packed program of nine events, sanctioned by the American Motorcycle Association, will be offered at the Route 40 track on Sunday afternoon, starting promptly at 1 p.m.

The attractive card is being sponsored by the Little Heiskell Motorcycle Club of Hagerstown, and it is expected that thousands of followers of the daring sport will be on hand for the action.

Jerry Mullines, president of the Little Heiskell group, said today that advance entries indicate that well over 100 riders will be in competition in the three different classes—expert, amateur and novice.

"Our race will follow right on the heels of the July 4th motorcycle card in Frederick," Mullines pointed out, "and most all of the riders who race in Frederick will come to Hagerstown the next day."

At least two Hagerstown riders will compete for a share of the purse money on Sunday afternoon. They are Marvin Twigg and Paul Kitchen, both of whom have fared very well on the motorcycle racing circuit this season.

Twigg has won close to 10 feature races in the expert class this year and is fast becoming recognized as one of the top cycle pilots in the Eastern part of the United States.

Before suffering a leg injury during a recent race at Winchester, Kitchen chalked up several impressive triumphs in the amateur class. He is now completely recovered from the injury and anxiously looking forward to riding before the home fans.

Both Twigg and Kitchen will be riding Birmingham Small Arms (BSA) British cycles in Sunday's races here.

Little Heiskell's 1st races were at the speedway, but that would soon change.

111

Don Twigg at Little Heiskell, 1968

Gary Nixon at Little Heiskell

The man with the cigar, racing the grand national champion is unidentified, but has been suggested as either Jake Bemisderfer or Jack Mercer.

Willie Moye and Chuck Palmgren at Little Heiskell 1965.
Note the brakes allowed for TT racing.

A teenager on a Honda Cub, being passed by the GNC champ.

These photos were made during a practice day at Little Heiskell, but the old TT track held regularly scheduled AMA sanctioned races during the 1960's.

The club's track was located along the westside of the Conococheague Creek in the sharp bend of Cress Pond Road. Despite the track's demise nearly sixty years ago, it has only been on the most recent online satellite images that the scars of the old track have finally faded away. Little Heiskell was considered a "TT track." Instead of the usual flat oval, it included right turns and elevation changes. Not to the degree of scrambles or motocross, but decidedly different from a regular oval track. AMA specifies four categories for dirt tracks. [Flat Tracks] Miles, ½ miles, Short Tracks, and TT's.

Little Hieskell Motorcycle Club TT track in the 1960's

Mile and ½ mile tracks are self-explanatory, it being a reference to the distance involved in one complete lap around the oval. A "short track" is any oval track less than a ½ mile. Usually, from 1/10 to 3/8 mile. TT's as mentioned above must have at least one right turn and a "hill." The latter typically incorporating a "jump" at its brink. There is no specified length for a TT. Little Heiskell was roughly 1/3 mile. The track opened on July 3, 1960, as the second round in three days of sanctioned Maryland racing beginning at the Cumberland fairgrounds on Saturday the 2nd and culminating with the Frederick ½ mile on Monday the 4th. The club had 52 members in Hagerstown when it opened that day and drew riders from Ohio, New York, Pennsylvania, NJ, DE., MD., VA., and WV. The club also hosted Observed Trials events.

Trials (**not** *trails*) is a form of motorcycle sport where the rider must negotiate an extreme obstacle course. Unlike other forms of motorcycle sport, speed is not the object.

Instead, the goal is to obtain the lowest score. Riders are under constant scrutiny of an event judge who follows their progress, hence the *Observed* trails name. Events are held regardless of weather conditions.

Riders receive one point for every time they touch the ground for any reason. Successfully completing the difficult course without putting your foot down to maintain balance or avert a spill earns a perfect score of zero. Today the sport uses very specialized bikes designed specifically for it. During the 1960's though, riders can be assumed to have shown up at Little Heiskell's club grounds with basically any lightweight off-road style motorcycle.

There was also motocross in Washington County. In fact, the track was within the city limits of Hagerstown! In 1968 *"The Antietam Motorcycle Club."* Was organized by Leon Fearnow and Don Twigg. The club's track was off Howell Road between Mt. Aetna Road and Edgewood Drive. Having Fearnow, a respected member of the Hagerstown police department, as club president undoubtedly helped ease community relations for the noisy sport.

1st club president, Leon Fearnow (shorts & Yamaha Tee), conducting the pre-race rider's meeting.

Antietam Motorcycle Club's 2nd Moto-Cross (July 19) Was Even More Successful Than The First!

And once again we are thankful to all the people who made it possible. To our neighbors around "Antietam Moto-Sport Park," who have more than cooperated with our efforts to hold well-run events; to the newspaper, radio, and TV folks who helped us with advertising and publicity; for the invaluable service of Community Rescue, whose men and equipment guaranteed safety amid the excitement of racing; to the more than fifty motorcycle riders who competed with great talent and good sportsmanship; and most of all to the 700 sports fans who were our "customers," proving that Moto-Cross racing is "the most exciting sport on two wheels!" Our next Moto-Cross Race will be Sunday, August 2. We'd like to have every one of you back again!

As seen by this July 22, 1970 "thank you" ad in the Daily Mail paper, the track enjoyed an unprecedented welcome in Hagerstown.

MOTO-CROSS MOTO-CROSS

SUNDAY, MAY 23rd

"The BIG Sport of Motorcyclists"
at MOTO-SPORT PARK

Antietam Motorcycle Club Grounds
on Howell Road
GATES OPEN 11 A.M.
Practice Starts 12 Noon—Races Start 1 PM
American Motorcycle Association Sanctioned

Antietam Motorcycle Club alumni, former president and historian Jeff DeLauder has related that the original club property on Howell Road was personally leased by Leon Fearnow and Don Twigg. *"The original track was laid out and cut in by Billy Beard using his farm tractor. The 1 ½ mile course included a mudhole where a small spring emptied into the Antietam Creek along with numerous elevation changes."* When the track first opened, the entry fee was $2.00 with non-sanctioned racing for 125cc, 250cc and "open" classes. AMA sanction was soon obtained, and Antietam became a regular stop in mid-Atlantic racing circles.

Senior "B" Class coming off the line at the Antietam Track in Hagerstown, Md. . . . "Supporting the Sport" with the largest class all year at most local installations!!

Photo by Lawrence Hedges

"UP ON THE PEGS" IT'S MOTO-CROSS

THIS IS SOME OF THE MOST EXCITING COMPETITION ON 2 WHEELS

GATES OPEN 11 A.M. — PRACTICE 12 NOON — RACING STARTS 1 P.M.

SUNDAY – JUNE 3

The most exciting form of motorcycle racing, on a 1½ mile open field course with jumps, bumps, turns and the famous "mudhole"!

- THE TRACK HAS BEEN IMPROVED FOR SPECTATOR AND RIDER
- BIGGER TROPHIES AND PRIZES FOR AMATEURS AND EXPERTS!
- REFRESHMENTS ON THE GROUNDS
- 2 HEAT MINI BIKE RACE (Max. 80 c.c. and Age 13)

For further information contact:
ANTIETAM MOTORCYCLE CLUB, P. O. Box 1069, Hagerstown, Md. 21740, Phone (301) 733-9109.

120

ANTIETAM MOTORCYCLE CLUB
PRESENTS

1976   1976

A.M.A. SANCTIONED
MOTO-CROSS

SAT FEB 28	4 HR. HARE SCRAMBLE	
SUN MAR 21	4 HR. HARE SCRAMBLE	
SAT APR 3	MOTO-X	
SAT APR 17	MOTO-X	
SUN MAY 2	MOTO-X YOUTH & 125	
SUN MAY 9	MOTO-X	
SAT MAY 22	MOTO-X YOUTH, 250 & POWDER PUF	
SAT JUN 5	MOTO-X YOUTH CHAMPIONSHIP	
SAT JUN 19	MOTO-X	
SUN JUL 18	MOTO-X SEMI-PRO, A & B ONLY (EXPERT POINT EVENT)	
SAT AUG 7	MOTO-X	
SUN AUG 22	MOTO-X	
SAT SEP 4	MOTO-X	
SAT SEP 11	MOTO-X SEMI-PRO	
SAT OCT 2	MOTO-X	
SAT OCT 16	MOTO-X	
SAT OCT 30	MOTO-X	
SUN NOV 7	4 HR. HARE SCRAMBLE	

STREET RIDER EVENTS

MAY 31   SECRET MILEAGE RUN to York, Pa. Motorcycle Race

JUL 11   POKER RUN

AUG 1   POKER RUN
AUG 29   POKER RUN

SEP 19   POKER RUN

SIGN-UP 9:30 A.M. ▬▬▬▬ **PRACTICE 11:00 A.M.** ▬▬▬▬ **RACING STARTS 12:00 NOON**

THE MOST EXCITING FORM OF MOTORCYCLE RACING, ON A 1 1/2 MILE OPEN FIELD COURSE WITH JUMPS, BUMPS AND TURNS

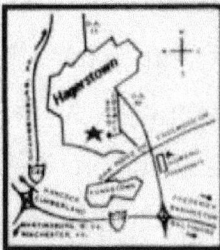

·RIDERS

125cc, 250cc, OPEN CLASSES. A,B,C.
MUFFLERS REQUIRED
DISTRICT 7 POINTS

For further information contact:
ANTIETAM MOTORCYCLE CLUB,
P. O. Box 1069, Hagerstown, Md. 21740
Phone (301) 797-8686

WELCOME TO ANTIETAM MOTO-SPORT PARK

LENGTH APPROX. 1.5 MILES
ELEVATION CHANGE 50'

ALL EVENTS A.M.A. SANCTIONED

SPECTATOR RULES:

1. No Alcoholic Beverages
2. No Practice Before 12:00 Noon
3. All Children Must Be Accompanied
   By an Adult (21)
4. Keep All Unnecessary Motorcycles
   Off The Track

His   Hers

Sign Up Bus

Radio Truck

PITS
COMPATION MACHINERY ONLY

HOWELL ROAD TO RT. 40

Start Line

FINISH

Score Shack

Jump

Spectator Parking In
This Area

ANTIETAM CREEK

Sand Trap

The Mud Hole

Drop Off

Ravine

Incline & Jump

Big Natural Jump

Jump

Dead End

ANTIETAM MOTORCYCLE CLUB INC.
BOX 1069   HAGERSTOWN, MARYLAND 21740

A clerical error in late 1973 resulted in the club's 74 race schedule moving from Sundays to Saturdays. As luck would turn out, due to the fuel crisis, gas stations were closed nationally on Sundays during 1974 precluding much travel on those days. It was a stroke of luck unintentionally benefitting the club's unplanned schedule change.

122

Antietam could be a tough course!

Antietam MC Club outing in 1969

As briefly touched upon in the introduction to this section, the late Leon Fearnow, was a Hagerstown city police officer. He had been the club president since its founding. Leon was a *BIG* man who commanded respect just by his presence. Whether pertaining to his duties as a Hagerstown police detective, or running the weekly rider's meeting, when Leon spoke, people shut up and listened.

That big tough guy appearance was a ruse - *usually*. Leon Fearnow, as attention getting as that gruff deep voice might seem, and as big and intimidating as he might appear to strangers, could be one of the nicest people anyone could wish to meet. In retirement, Leon ran a popular take-out restaurant on Franklin Street in downtown Hagerstown, *"Leon's Hoagie Shop."* A specialty was chicken barbequed right there on the sidewalk (after he got *THAT* straightened out with the city!). The smell of Leon's chicken was a welcomed addition to the usual smells downtown and attracted customers for blocks around. Leon was in business for thirteen years, but it was only the top quality of his food that kept the business profitable – marginally. That was because Leon gave away almost as much food to those who couldn't afford it as what he sold to paying customers. As well, during those 13 years, the night shifts at local police and fire and rescue agencies ate a lot of free chicken, allegedly *"left over at closing time"* and personally delivered by Leon Fearnow who knew the challenges of working overnights.

I had the pleasure of knowing Leon personally. Just one of the thousands who did. I've known few men who earned so much respect by his actions. My own lasting mental image of him will always be bouncing along as he mowed the grass at the Hagerstown FOP lodge – the mower running *wide open*. Leon shirtless and smiling. His jostling, hefty size and happy grin reminded me of Buddha. In retrospect, perhaps more fitting than originally thought.

Antietam Motorcycle Club's *second* President, Jeff DeLauder, can tell the story of succession into the post-73 season better than I can do it justice.

"The first meeting of the new year was held at President Leon Fearnow's home in January. We were down to about 10 members and Leon announced that he had been promoted to Detective and working nights would preclude him from being active with the Club. He asked for a volunteer to take over as President. Being just 18 and not of sound mind, I reluctantly volunteered. Leon attended the first race to show me "the ropes" and bid me good luck. (Little did I know this was to be a long-term assignment.) I also soon found out we were in debt and owed money to several local vendors. We owned a set of flags and a flag-stand and an old blue bus with no engine.

The next meeting was held in my van on March 17th at the track. There we decided the down-hill start had to go. We re-arranged the track layout, moved the bus and concession stands and ran a loop of the track behind the rocks. Influenced by the '74 Daytona SX, I asked Steve Pearl (Henson & Son, Inc.) to dig me two alligator pits in the straight in front of the rocks. He did, we used them briefly until a downpour filled them with water drained from the front field.

At the same time, we began to gain new members that were motocross focused. We pulled through and acquired a roll of surgical hose for our rubber band start. The Saturday races were poorly attended but were a blessing in disguise as I was still learning. Six classes, times three motos each, plus a "mini-bike" class, and we still finished by about 5:00-5:30 PM. Good times." - Jeff DeLauder former club president

Antietam Moto-sport track

Antietam Motorcycle Club
Starts Roadside Cleanup

Hagerstown's newest sporting organization sponsored a roadside cleanup service this morning along Dual Highway to Mt. Aetna Rd. and Howell Rd.

The Antietam Motorcycle Club was organized early this year and presently boasts of 30 members. Men, women and juniors are invited to join if their interest leans to motorbikes or cycles.

The group placed trash barrels along the highway with markers for motorists to deposit litter. The cleanup activity is part of Earth Day activities held locally the first part of this week.

Monthly cleanup tours are planned by group. Their objective, besides keeping the roadsides clean, is to impress people that motorcycle clubs are interested in public service.

An affiliate of the American Motorcycle Association, the Antietam Motorcycle Club has two professional racers in its membership, Eddie Adkins and Roy Bowers.

In addition to a complete range of events of road riders, trial rides, field meets and motor - cross races, the organization is also planning a rider education program and safety training in cooperation with the Hagerstown City Police, Maryland State Police, driver education experts and the Washington County Safety Committee.

Club officers are president Leon Fearnow, vice-president Don Twigg, secretary Bill Clopper and treasurer Bob Moats. Interested people wishing further information on joining the club may write the officers, Antietam Motorcycle Club, 2369 Pennsylvania Ave., Hagerstown, Maryland 21740.

This clipping from 1970 helps explain why Antietam MC enjoyed community acceptance as a different kind of motorcycle club.

127

Motorcycle racing—Twigg's easy choice

By BOB FLEENOR

Mike Twigg could have continued being a pretty good baseball player, a good football player, and a very good motorcycle racer all at the same time. Or, he could become a professional motorcycle racer.

The decision was an easy one to make for the South Hagerstown High senior.

Mike grew up around motorcycles. His father, Don, is a former flat-track racer, who runs a cycle dealership in Hagerstown. Mike had the talent to jump from Class C (novice) to Class A (expert amateur) in his first summer of serious competitive racing.

In January, one month after his 17th birthday, Mike will apply to the American Motorcycle Association for his professional card. He will become one of some 3,000 pros chasing prize money on the national motocross circuit.

Mike is a versatile athlete who played varsity baseball at South High and was a member of the local Pony League all-stars in 1975. He played two seasons at linebacker for the Rebel football team, but didn't come back out this year.

"It all boiled down to deciding what I was going to do," Mike said. "It's like those athletes in high school and college who are good in two or three sports. When it comes time to go pro they have to decide on one or the other.

"This (cycle racing) is more of an opportunity

MIKE TWIGG...motorcycle man

Antietam Moto-Sport Park

There was also drag racing.

```
┌─────────────────────────────────────────┐
│ ┌─────────────────────────────────────┐ │
│ │                                     │ │
│ │     HAGERSTOWN  DRAGWAY             │ │
│ │         - OPENING -                 │ │
│ │     NEW 1/4 MI. DRAG STRIP          │ │
│ │            LOCATED                  │ │
│ │     6 Miles East on U.S. Rt. 40     │ │
│ │     RACES EVERY SUNDAY              │ │
│ │           Beginning                 │ │
│ │         SEPT. 3 RD.                 │ │
│ │   Mason-Dixon Timing Assoc. officiating │
│ │        N.H.R.A. Sanctioned          │ │
│ │   Elwood Grimm        Ralph W. Poe  │ │
│ │      Promoter          Announcer    │ │
│ └─────────────────────────────────────┘ │
└─────────────────────────────────────────┘
```

Sept. 3, 1961, grand opening of Mason Dixon Dragway

[ad reflects original name]

Elwood Grimm was a "repurposed auto parts dealer" from the Hagerstown area. In plainer language, he ran a junk yard at Chewsville.

That doesn't sound very flattering today, but in the 50's and 60's, the local junk yard was often the first stop when car repair parts were needed by DIY mechanics. Automobile tinkerers, customizers, and innovators viewed the junk yard as a treasure trove. This of course brought Mr. Grimm into regular contact with everyone in the local hot rod community, which at that time was approaching the all-time peak of its popularity.

129

Drag races had ceased being held at the speedway and local speedsters were getting into regular trouble practicing their hobby on the public roads. The goal of the police, although unlikely to be attainable, was to shut down the activity. Grimm's junk yard thrived on the racer's business.

-- Hot Rod --
DRAG RACES
HAGERSTOWN SPEEDWAY
SUNDAY, 1 P. M.
3,000 Seats at $1.00
Children Free

1952 ad for drag races at the speedway

With a keen eye for opportunity, Elwood Grimm laid out the drag strip in 1960 right beside U.S. 40, six miles east of Hagerstown. The Hagerstown Speedway coincidentally, is an equal distance west of town. Construction was finished in the summer of 1961 and the grand opening was held over Labor Day weekend with a huge crowd of curious and anxious fans.

Racing was held weekly on Sunday afternoons for decades. Mason Dixon Dragway is still in operation and motorcycles continue to be regular participants with a few motorcycle only events through the years. The name has changed slightly over time, but Mason Dixon still holds a 70's-esk nostalgia like few other racing venues.

DRAG RACES

SUNDAY 2 P.M.

TRIPLE FEATURE

--Run Off For Penny's 500--

Collins & Hickman National Champion Camaro	VS.	Dick Hill Super Stock Dodge
Barbara Isern Galloping Grapes	VS.	Nelson Parker Chevy Gasser

Complete 2nd Racing Program for All Classes

MOTORCYCLE DRAG RACES

Mason Dixon Dragway

Rt. 40 -- 6 mi. East of Hagerstown

Hagerstown Daily Mail, Aug. 22, 1969

Motorcycle Racing Set
For Mason-Dixon Track

The first annual Maryland State motorcycle drag racing championship sponsored by the Maryland Motorcycle Club is scheduled for Sunday, Nov. 5, at the Mason-Dixon Dragway.

Five events in 27 /classes will be held for stock and modified bikes of all types. The events will include a slalom run, ¼-mile drag race, LeMans start race, wheelstand contest and a team relay race.

Trophies for winners and runners up will be awarded in all classes in addition to cash prizes for overall winners.

More than 200 cyclists are expected to compete in the all day program including world record holder for the ¼-mile drag, Sonny Routt, of Arlington, Va. Routt drives a twin engined Triumph motorcycle which hits a top speed of more than 145 miles per hour in the ¼-mile.

Time trials for all classes begin at 10 a.m. with final eliminations starting at 2 p.m.

Rules and entry information may be obtained by calling Event Director at area code 703, 560-4331. The Mason-Dixon Dragway is located 6 miles east of Hagerstown on U.S. Route 40.

Oct. 28, 1967, Maryland State championship

motorcycle drag race.

132

Sanctioned motorcycle racing had been absent in Washington County since 2015. In 2021, after several years of exploring ideas by local enthusiasts, motorcycle racing returned not only to the Hagerstown area, but after more than 75 years, to the *Washington County Fair*.

The leadership of AMA district 7 worked out a partnership with the fair board to stage a short-track motorcycle race on the first day of the fair. Days of groundwork were invested to prepare the track and by Saturday morning the ground crew had turned it into a beautifully prepped, smooth 1/10-mile oval. More than 50 riders showed up and practiced but a severe thunderstorm flooded the track and cancelled racing before heat races could begin. At the time of writing, motorcycle racing **is again scheduled for July 2022,** and it is hoped it once again becomes the annual fair tradition it once was.

WashCo Ag Expo & Fair
July 16, 2022 Practice & qualifying in afternoon RACING begins @ 7:00

Admission $15
(6 & under free)

Fair Exhibits
FREE
Today Only

7313 Sharpsburg Pike
Boonsboro, MD.

Exit 29 from I-70 onto
Rt.65 S. 6 mi. to
FAIRGROUND

50 Years
A.M.A. DISTRICT 7
MD - DC - DE
1966 - 2016

10 CLASSES
pre-teen to seniors
Modern & Vintage
Riders from
throughout the
Mid-Atlantic region

Sponsored & Staffed by
AMA Dist. 7 officials

MOTORCYCLE RACES
1/10th mile prepared clay track

AMERICAN MOTORCYCLIST ASSOCIATION

Clubs

MOTOR CLUB DINES

The Motorcycle Club of Hagerstown took dinner at the Lee House, Smithsburg, Tuesday night. Those present were: Albert Miner, president; Theo. Knox, Chester Delphey, Clarence Feigley, F. Lester Miner, John W. Smith, Clarence Young, S. Rock, Terry McDaley, Daniel Fessler, Walter Stoddard, Melvin Shipley, Paul Reisner, Ernest Show, W. F. Ankeney, Colvin R. Waddell.

Hagerstown, "Morning Herald," June 8 1929

As touched upon repeatedly, there have been many local motorcycle associations, both formal and informal, throughout the region. Motorcycling is a unique activity in that while practiced individually, it invariably draws people together.

Many motorcycle activities involve contests in some form. Such activities of course, require various participants, but the gregarious aspects of motorcycles reach far beyond races.

Many bikes only have a single seat. But even those designed for passengers, are not very accommodating to interaction between the riders. Modern electronics have been integrated into helmets and wearable devices allowing voice communication between riders on the same bike as well as other members of a group riding together. Yet, I've never heard anyone say, "*I sure am glad I can talk to people while riding my motorcycle.*"

The emotional peace of riding a motorcycle, even as a passenger *or* while involved in operations simultaneously requiring use of all four hands and feet, is hard to explain to non-riders. Perhaps that is why we enjoy each other's company so much. We understand each other.

Whether through organized clubs. Through organizations to oversee other activities, or simply informal friendships formed through and maintained by a common interest, motorcycles are a uniting factor.

Racing, that single activity running through everything motorcycle, was soon after its origin determined to need a central governing organization. In Sept. 1903 several northeastern U.S. motorcycle enthusiasts formed the **Federation of American Motorcyclists**, in part, to create organized rules and standards for motorcycle racing, but also to advocate for motorcyclist concerns.

F.A.M. very quickly became a national organization and attained its goal of drawing all reputable motorcycle events under its guiding hand. The aim for F.A.M., rather than dictation of rules was standardization of them assuring that the best (period) safety standards were observed and applied.

F.A.M.'s greatest handicap was that it was a completely volunteer organization. There were no paid officers and operating budgets depended upon meager membership fees. Despite hundreds of thousands of race *fans* in the nineteen-teens most were not motorcyclists themselves. Not all who were, joined. By 1919, the burden of F.A.M. operations exceeded that which could be freely given by volunteers and the organization closed its doors.

Federation of American Motorcyclists logo

137

With close to 100 motorcycle companies in the U.S. at the time, another organization had taken shape in November 1916. The **Motorcycle and Allied Trades Association** (M&ATA) was a trade group of manufactures, dealers, and other industry partners. While better funded, with company employee representatives paid to attend meetings, it was considerably more successful than the F.A.M.. But the M&ATA represented the industry instead of the users.

M&ATA recognized the need for an organization to oversee racing and tried to assist F.A.M. through its last few years to no avail. For three years (1920-1923) M&ATA was the only sanctioning body for motorcycle racing. In 1924, M&ATA created a sub-agency representing motorcycle users, **The American Motorcyclist's Association**.

AMA was supposed to be an independent organization, but since it was primarily funded and totally operated by M&ATA, there were frequent accusations of bias whenever some decision appeared to favor one brand or team over another. Whether the accusations were founded or not, by 1930 there were only two manufactures left to argue about. Twenty years later, that number would drop to one but about that time, imported brands were also allowed representation in M&ATA / AMA via their American importers.

"Goodbye, Strap-Hangers"

Home in a Jiffy!

WHILE the crowds wait and scramble to get aboard jammed street cars, you breeze home on your Motorcycle

See the new models at:

J. J. CONNER
771 South Potomac street

LAMBERT'S MCY. SHOP
32 East Franklin street

E. B. SMITH
248 Winter street

and all other authorized motorcycle dealers.

—a quick, pleasant jaunt in the fresh air, that chases all the glooms out of your system and gets you home in time for early supper, with an appetite like a kid's.

You actually save money over carfare, too, counting time saved. And think of the sport you'll have with your Motorcycle on Saturday afternoons and Sundays.

If you want to travel independently, swiftly, economically, comfortably—"Do it with a Motorcycle."

MOTORCYCLE & ALLIED TRADES ASSOCIATION

Do it with a Motorcycle

¼ page M.&A.T.A. Ad in the Hagerstown Daily Mail, May 1921

AMA was still operated by the Motorcycle and Allied Trade Association into the 1960's when it experienced push back from some members. Particularly racers and those behind the scenes of racing felt they were taken for granted by an organization that did not give them a voice in its decisions pertaining directly to them.

The result of this was the complete separation of AMA from M&ATA. The resulting new AMA was operated by a paid chairman and 25 AMA member Congressmen. The chairman handled the day-to-day business but answered to the congress. The Congressmen were one, from each of the 25 regional districts around the United States. Each being elected by their respective districts for two-year terms. A separate Competition Congress had control of racing oversight. Made up of the 25 congressmen, six professional racers elected by the licensed riders, and several industry representatives.

On March 11th, 1966, Bob Myers (formerly of Downsville), Bob Rudy and Howard Whittington of Washington D.C., officially incorporated **"MOTORCYCLING UNLIMITED, of AMA DISTRICT 7, Inc."** and so became the founding officers of AMA district 7 with responsibility for Maryland, Delaware, and the District of Columbia.

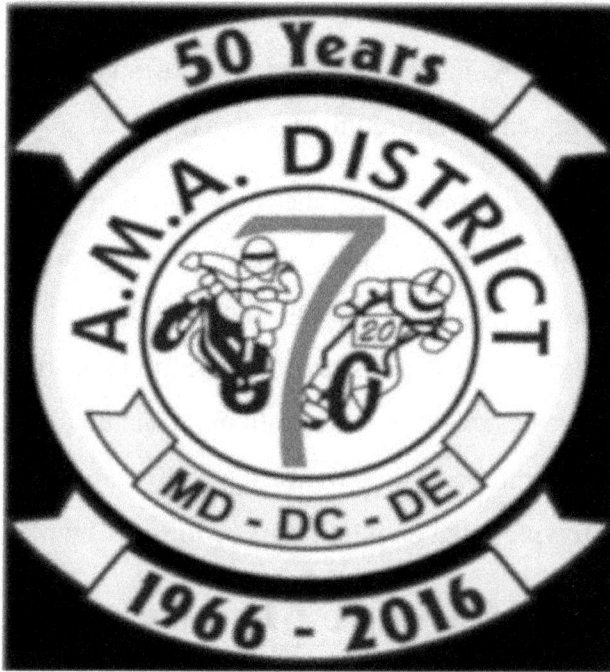

50 Years
A.M.A. DISTRICT 7
MD - DC - DE
1966 - 2016

While AMA is best known for overseeing racing, it is actually a full-service rider organization providing many other support services for every type of motorcycle user. The stated goal of the new district seven, as enumerated in its legal incorporating documents was, *"to engage in, carry on and coordinate motorcycling activities, projects and events which shall enhance the sport of motorcycling."*

The AMA congress is a truly democratic organization fully overseen by members who are motorcycle users rather than manufacturers and importers. After 50 years, it was a restoration of the lofty ideals of the all-user F.A.M.

That covers the broader national organizations. Closer to home, there have been numerous official motorcycle clubs, frequently referred to simply as "MC's."

Way back in chapter one is a faded photo of the **"Hagerstown Motorcycle Club"** making a stop in Hagerstown's square during an outing. During this early period there were various brand or location specific clubs. Most were based in the metropolitan areas due to the sheer number of motorcyclists living there. Eventually though, Hagerstown gained enough riders to form its own club.

Motorcycle Club On A Tour To Caverns

Forty-five members of the Hagerstown Motorcycle Club in company with twenty-five members of the Martinsburg Motorcycle Club made a one-day tour to Shenandoah Caverns. Va., Sunday. The trip from this city and return required six hours running time which covered 180 miles through the beautiful and historical valley of Virginia. The Motorcycle Club reports a pleasant trip both in route and thru the Saverns. Many local people also motored to Shenandoah Caverns from this city also on Sunday. Several hours were spent in the Caverns by members of the Motorcycle Club. Mr. Ned Lambert and Mr. Dellinger had charge of the tour.

Morning Herald, August 8, 1923

MOTORCYCLE RUN.

The Baltimore Motorcycle Club, represented by twelve members made a run through Hagerstown yesterday. They returned to Baltimore via Frederick.

The Hagerstown Motorcycle Club made a run yesterday to Mercersburg. There were nine in the party.

Hagerstown Morning Herald September 25, 1911

PLANNING BIG THINGS.

Driving Club Getting Ready for the Opening Meet.

Big doings are being planned by the Driving Club for May 30, and every indication is that the first meet will be the largest and most successful ever held. There will be five different races in addition to the horse show, aeroplane flight and many other attractions. The airship, as stated before, will make three flights, and in one will race a motorcycle.

There will be a mule race, chariot race, motorcycle race and bicycle race, in which events cups will be awarded. The entries in the horse show are filling rapidly, and this will be one of the feat___ ___ the day.

John E. Wis___
___onal Asso___

Hagerstown Mail, May 10, 1912

143

Only eighteen years earlier, John Rowland had to travel to Frederick to buy a motorcycle. Forty-five *members* participating in a 180-mile ride on rough unpaved roads speaks to how much the sport had grown in a very short time. Add an additional 25 members from Martinsburg, WV, who joined them there and this was quite the group. That familiar name, Ned Lambert, Hagerstown's first motorcycle dealer, would be a long-time member of **The Hagerstown Motorcycle Club**.

Hagerstown MC outing along C&O Canal, 1919

The club was still active through World War II and when national racing resumed on February 22, 1947, four of the 21 members still riding with the Hagerstown club rode to the new Daytona beach racecourse as spectators.

There were still more than 20 members attending the 1948 *"annual banquet and meeting,"* where the coming

144

Hagerstown MC members "in camp" during an extended Gypsy Tour outing. Note wicker sidecar at left with wheel removed for repair.

year's activities were tentatively planned, but official accounts of the clubs' activities disappear from news reports after 1948. Many of the members named in the previous articles continue to appear in motorcycle news from Hagerstown for decades afterward. One of those named is Miller McDonald, then the Hagerstown Harley-Davidson dealer at 203 E. Washington Street who would return to Daytona in 1949 as a racer. The Hagerstown MC's clubhouse was then in the back of McDonald's Washington Street shop. There is no local news on results except that Mac was one of 46 to finish – out of 135 entries. Don Emde's "Daytona 200" book reveals that Mac finished a respectable 12th out of those 135 international entries.

145

Another pre-1920 Hagerstown MC outing at an unknown location.

As covered previously, in 1960 a new club formed in Hagerstown. The locally significant name of "*Little Heiskell* **MC**" was selected. Undoubtedly to the bewilderment of visiting racers.

A First

Motorcycle Races Open Tomorrow

A new racing sport, on motorcycles, will get underway in Washington County this weekend, starting tomorrow afternoon. Officials of the Little Heiskell Motorcycle Club have announced the opening of their racing oval near Broadfording.

Sanctioned by the American Motorcycle Association (AMA), nine events will be held tomorrow, three each in the ~~~~ ~ateur and exp~~~~
~ic

TT track racing debuts in July 1960

Motorcycle Club Slates Last Event

Motorcycle racing will hold the local sports spotlight this Sunday when the Little Heiskel Motorcycle Club holds its last race of the season on their T.T. track located on Cress Pond Road near Broadfording.

Novice amateur and expert riders from the eastern, central and some western states will be competing with local riders for the coveted trophies. Sanctioned by the American Motorcycle Association (AMA), the event has been classified as a Class "C" competition.

Time trails are scheduled to begin promptly at 1 p.m., with the starting flag dropping at 2 p.m. The present track record for one lap is 20.20 seconds is held by Dick Clark, Greenville, S.C., but one of Hagerstown's own competition riders, Paul Kitchem, who holds second fastest time, will endeavor to set a new record. Don Twigg, another Hagerstonian, is racing his first year of competition, and is following very rapidly in the steps of his brother, who thrilled local fans last year.

As a special added attraction a club uniform contest will be held, open to all motorcycle clubs, and participation is urged. Trophies will be awarded to the three best dressed clubs.

The club ground and track are most easily reached by driving west on U.S. Route 40 to Huyetts Crossroads, turn right on the Greencastle- Williamsport Road, turn left on Broadfording Road, and follow the signs (about 3½ miles).

This October 8, 1960 article announcing Little Heiskell's last race of the season makes the interesting announcement that this was Don Twigg's first year racing while mentioning brother Marvin's outstanding performance in previous years..

147

Eddie Adkins, at the 1964 Marlboro, MD road race.

Eddie Adkins, then a Hagerstown based professional racer, expert motorcycle builder and tuner was a prominent member of the Little Heiskell club. Little Heiskell was primarily a racing club, but news reports point to social activities besides the regular AMA sanctioned races held at their property on Cress Pond Road. Little Heiskell stopped holding races about 1970 and sold their property on September 5, 1972.

Former club president and charter member, Jeff DeLauder places 1968 as the year **Antietam Motorcycle Club** was first formed. According to period news reports, April 1970 is when they officially held their first race at the club's "*Antietam Moto-Sport Park*" on Howell Road. The paper reported 30 active members at that time.

The club was organized by Hagerstown police detective Leon Fearnow with considerable support from his friend, local businessman and pro racer, Donald Twigg. Don of course was the son of Hagerstown's premier motorcycle dealer H. William Twigg of Twigg's Cycles.

Don Twigg, Hagerstown, at 1965 Marlboro, MD road races.

Antietam MC caught the crest of the MX wave and rode it high and wide throughout the 70's, 80's and 90's. Unfortunately, as is a much too familiar story these days, the home of Antietam MC, once a 221-acre farm, became prime development real estate.

Despite the good examples demonstrated by the club as considerate neighbors and conscientious community members, the expanding city just was not compatible with the *BRAAAAP, BRAAAAP* of five-to-six-hour long weekly motorcycle races. President Jeff DeLauder places 2003 as the official demise of Antietam MC.

ANTIETAM
MOTORCYCLE CLUB

1982 — SCHEDULE OF EVENTS

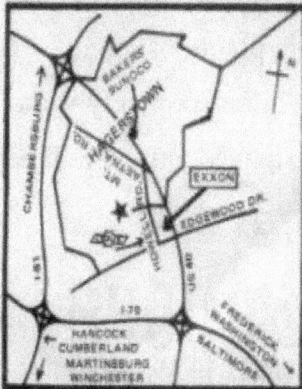

OFF - ROAD COMPETITION EVENTS
— Rain or Shine —

	MONTH	DAY	EVENT
	MARCH	21	HARE SCRAMBLES (Semi-Pro)
3	APRIL	25	MOTO-CROSS (Semi-Pro, Am. & Youth)
★	MAY	2	MOTO-CROSS (AMATEUR ONLY)
3	MAY	23	MOTO-CROSS (Semi-Pro, Am. & Youth)
3	JUNE	27	MOTO-CROSS (Semi-Pro, Am. & Youth)
3	JULY	18	MOTO-CROSS (Semi-Pro, Am. & Youth)
3	SEPT.	19	MOTO-CROSS (Semi-Pro, Am. & Youth)
3	OCT.	3	MOTO-CROSS (Semi-Pro, Am. & Youth)
★	OCT.	24	MOTO-CROSS (AMATEUR ONLY)
	NOV.	7	HARE SCRAMBLES (Semi-Pro)

"★"	DISTRICT 7 EXPERT POINTS RACE
"3"	THREE WHEELERS

OBSERVED TRIALS: JUNE 5th & 6th (Two-Day) & AUGUST 8, 1982
NOTE: All Observed Trials events at Antietam Club Grounds are sponsored by Central Maryland Trials Association (301) 775-7209.

Take U.S. 40W Exit (32B), off I-70 to 1st traffic light and follow signs to track on Howell Road.

ROAD RIDING EVENTS

APRIL	4	POKER RUN
JUNE	6	POKER RUN
AUG.	8	POKER RUN
SEPT.	12	POKER RUN
OCT.	10	POKER RUN

All Road Riding Events begin at BAKERS' SUNOCO on U.S. 40 at Antietam Creek East of Hagerstown.

SIGN-IN 12:30 to 1 P.M.
OPEN TO AMA & NON-AMA RIDERS & PASSENGERS

AMA
AMERICAN MOTORCYCLIST ASSOCIATION

ALL EVENTS AMA & DIST. 7 SANCTIONED
NEW RIDERS ALWAYS WELCOME
92dbA NOISE LIMIT ENFORCED
3-Wheeler Classes: 0-125, 126-200, 201-250cc

GATE OPENS 8:30 A.M.
SIGN-Up 9 A.M.
RIDERS MEETING 10:30 A.M.
PRACTICE 11:00 - 11:55
RACES START 12 NOON

Antietam Motorcycle Club, 455 N. Colonial Drive, Hagerstown, Md. 21740

(301) 797-8686 (9 A.M. - 9 P.M.) 797-1607

151

In 1972 the board of directors for Antietam MC voted after considerable discussion to build a scrambles track at Antietam Moto Sport Park in the space along Howell Road between the road and the moto track. Little Heiskel was no longer holding races and their property was sold later that same year. The Winchester VA scrambles track was attracting attention and so with plenty of room, Antietam planned to give it a try. Interest quickly waned however and the track never materialized although three events appear on the 72 schedule.

A.M.A. SANCTIONE[D]

APRIL 16 Moto-Cros[s]
MAY 7 Moto-Cros[s]
MAY 21 Moto-Cros[s]
JUNE 25 Moto-Cros[s]
JULY 9 Scramble[s]
AUGUST 13 Scramble[s]
SEPTEMBER 10 Scramble[s]
SEPTEMBER 24 Moto-Cros[s]
OCTOBER 8 Moto-Cros[s]
OCTOBER 22 Moto-Cros[s]

ANTIETAM MOTORCYCLE CLUB PRESENTS

MOTO-CROSS

GATE OPEN 11:00 A.M. ▬▬▬ PRACTICE 12:00 NOON ▬▬▬ RACING STARTS 1:00 P.[M.]

THE MOST EXCITING FORM OF MOTORCYCLE RACING, ON A 1 MILE OPEN FIELD COURSE WITH JUMPS, BUMPS, TURNS AND TH[E] FAMOUS "MUDHOLE"!

RIDERS

BIGGER TROPHIES AND PRIZES FOR AMATEUR[S] AND EXPERTS!
125cc, 250cc, OPEN CLASSES. 3 HEATS EACH.
MUFFLERS REQUIRED
DISTRICT POINTS GIVEN!

For further information contact:
ANTIETAM MOTORCYCLE CLUB, P.O. Box 1069, Hagerstown, Md. 217[40]
Phone (301) 797-7133

152

In the late 70's a brand-new MC was chartered. Not merely a new club but a completely new type of club!

A May 1978 article in *"Cycling East"* announced not only the formation of the new club but that it had been officially chartered by AMA. Club activities would have AMA (Dist. 7) sanction and be eligible for applicable points. It was the debut of an ambitious idea to promote both the sport and motorcycling in general among those most likely to embrace it, teenagers.

It was also hoped to make it safer for everyone, but especially newcomers, which the club hoped to attract. In many ways SMC was an extension of the existing Antietam MC mantra of being a community-oriented club. Making motorcycling more acceptable and legitimate as a sport and those involved more engaged as community members in a genuine, *publicly recognized* sport.

With origins like so much from the 70's in California, in 1975 the concept got a massive kickstart when riders from 50 California schools competed in an event during the Super Cross at the Los Angeles Coliseum. Originally, with support from Yamaha, the concept of Vic Wilson, a promoter at Saddleback Park where much of the footage for the iconic 70's moto film *"On Any Sunday"* was filmed, high school moto cross received world-wide attention. Predictably of course, teenagers in as many places around the globe thought it was a great idea.

The attraction among riders was natural. For the adult proponents it offered a unique avenue to engage a segment that can often be... well, less than devoted to academics. Involvement in an organized activity, like all school activities, carried the burden of maintaining behavior and performance standards. The abundance of dirt bikes in the hands of California kids, and especially southern California made the idea sound very appealing.

It was widely accepted in California and gradually spread throughout the west coast region and with varying degrees of success, throughout the country. But by 1978 it was still a largely untried and unfamiliar concept when the idea was pitched in District 7.

The *SERIOUS* discussions leading to D7 board acceptance of SMC as a legitimate effort.

The organization's goals as stated by Betsy Sanders, the adult supervisor for the club, were to.

Bring greater recognition to the sport through student participation; give training and instruction to first-time racers; develop ability and desire in the sport; emphasize physical fitness and athletic ability; attempt to get moto-cross adopted as an official "high-school sport." Ms

Sanders also expressed a desire to bring motorcycle awareness, safety, and operation instruction into the schools as part of the existing driver's education curriculum [which was then a high-school class].

Certainly, some lofty and admirable ideals. At the time there were already more than 15 participating schools listed throughout Maryland and Virginia and several events had already been held. The most recent was at White Oaks MX Park at Fredericksburg, VA. Before the day's racing began, the Scholastic Moto Crossers were led on a track walk by Pro racer Steve Robertson and given personal instruction on how to handle each element of the course.

Betsy concluded her Cycling East report with a plea to enrolled and potential club members to attend and *participate* in club functions and activities with the revelation of already diminishing attendance. That is perhaps the most ambitious of any goal regarding teenagers. At that age, interests are often varied and fleeting. The appeal for participation was a harbinger of things to come as the organization unfortunately proved to be short lived.

There is of course another kind of motorcycle club. Frequently referred to as *"outlaw clubs,"* the term originally, like so much in motorcycling, stems from racing. In its purest form, an outlaw club originally meant one not affiliated with the AMA. Hence, not bound by the association's "laws." Even today, races which are not sanctioned by AMA are still referred to as "outlaw races." This explanation though, is not to be confused with the present understanding of an outlaw club.

Today, *"outlaw clubs"* refers to those with a reputation, whether deserved or not, for not observing the rules of polite society. People are frequently viewed as potential or suspected criminals for mere association with such groups. Much of the perception and for some, attraction, is based in Hollywood's dramatic portrayals.

There are several national OMCs familiar to most people. One of them has deep roots in Maryland and hence, its members are not a totally unfamiliar sight on local roads.

Similarly, there have been other lesser OMCs which have come and gone through the years. One of them caused a brief stir in 1968. Hagerstown police chief Grayson Wingfield's comment that the Kamikazi's had *"seen too many Hell's Angles movies"* is a timely characterization of Hollywood's role in both the perception and attraction of outlaw clubs for some people.

Swastikas Spoil Its Image

Kamikazi Motorcycle Club Falls On Hard Times With Police, Public

By PHIL EBERSOLE

The Kamikazi Motorcycle Club has fallen on hard times. Club members have drawn a lot of hostile attention from passers-by during the past few weeks because of several members who wear the Nazi swastika emblem.

The club has drawn the hostile attention of the Hagerstown Police Department because of an incident in the Jonathan St. area two weeks ago.

And now the club is being turned out of its quarters on W. Lee St., and may disband, its leaders say.

Chief of Police Grayson Wigfield said the club is composed of a lot of people who have seen too many "Hell's Angels" movies for their own good. He said he has received a lot of complaints about Kamikazi motorcyclists making nuisances of themselves.

On Jonathan St.

On Sunday, April 7, he said, he received a complaint about a group of Kamikazi motorcyclists in the Jonathan St. area, making passes at people with their motorcycles, and forcing them to jump out of the street onto the curb. (Club members deny doing this.)

On the following Monday, Wig-some fellow club members, and came back with a gang, said Wigfield. Young Negro men emerged, too, and started to form a group, Wigfield said.

Nothing happened, said the police chief, because Hagerstown policemen cleared the motorcyclists, took them down to the First Hose Company firehall, and gave them a thorough lecturing.

"They admitted they were in the wrong," Wigfield said, "and said they wouldn't do it again."

Bad Image

The president of the club is Richard Churchey, 44, and he feels the club has gotten a bad image.

As he describes it, the club is basically no different from Washington County's other motorcycle clubs. They race on dirt tracks and on obstacle courses in the mountains. They take excursions as a club, and they race their cycles around abandoned quarries. Once they tried to run their motorcycles up to Black Rock from the steep side of the mountain.

There are a lot of motorcycle racing trophies in the club building. Most of them are his.

Churchey said the club started about two years ago, first for his friends and relations and then for a broader membership.name, he said, because motorcycle-riding is a dangerous sport and because most of them ride Japanese motorcycles.

Motorcycle riding is a challenging sport, requiring skill, knowledge, quick thinking and steady nerves. Churchey thinks that involving the members in this sport has helped to keep them off the street and out of trouble.

The club, he said, has strict rules, including no drinking on the premises. Among the members there has been one with a traffic ticket, he said.

Some Fighting

As other members join in the discussion, however, it comes out that members now and then get involved in fighting scrapes. As they see it, it is always the other fellow who is the aggressor — somebody picking on them because they are motorcycle riders.

Doesn't he think the swastika emblem invites trouble? Churchey observed mildly that most club members don't wear the emblem, and he wishes the rest wouldn't either.

The most conspicuous member of the club is his step-brother, John Churchey, 32, who wears a gleaming, silver, German-type helmet, a jacket with a large swastika and the wordHe added that he has had a lot of trouble from motorists who try to crowd motorcyclists off the road, either because they don't like them or because they don't notice them. Since he has started dressing up as a movie villain, he said, motorists notice him and steer clear of him.

Danged Bum

"They don't respect you unless you look like a danged bum," he said.

Doesn't he see anything wrong with wearing a Nazi swastika? "The Bible says, 'Forgive thine enemies,'" he said, "and the Germans were our enemies."

Wigfield's view is different. "Any SOB that wears a swastika ought to be deported," he said.

There is no law against wearing swastikas. Hagerstown policemen are, however, under orders to haul in any Kamikazi motorcyclist if—but only if—he breaks a law or creates a disturbance.

So far the Kamikazi motorcyclists have been minding their Ps and Qs, and they have had no more trouble.

May Disband

The problem of finding new quarters is more serious. With out a place to meet and work on

"In the late 1950's and early 60's the image of the American motorcycle rider, in cartoons, fiction, and motion pictures was a sub-human deviate. Either a sullen loner or a hotheaded punk who rode with gangs which specialized in terrorizing small towns.

Marlon Brando, in the movie "The Wild One" set the pattern for a generation of media misconceptions of the folks who preferred to sit astride their machines rather than inside them…"

Thus began a ½ page feature article on motorcycles in the Sept. 5, 1972, *Daily Mail* by Bob Maginnis [Bob would eventually be the H-M's chief editor] Bob emphasized

158

Hollywood's commercial exploitation of the unfair stereotype and tried to address the misperception with numerous positive examples. Particularly Antietam MC.

And Don't Call Them Hell's Angels

Growing Numbers Of Motorcyclists Found On Washington County Roads

By ROBERT MAGINNIS

In the late 1950's and early '60's, the image of the American motorcycle rider, in cartoons, fiction and motion pictures was a sub-human deviate, either a sullen loner or a hot-headed punk who rode with gangs which specialized in terrorizing small towns.

Marlon Brando, in the movie "The Wild One," set the pattern for a generation of media misconceptions of the folks who preferred to sit astride their machines rather than inside them.

But in 1961, two Japanese companies, Honda and Yamaha, launched a television advertising campaign to reverse this image. Instead of grubby anthropoids wearing leather jackets and hanging around on growling two-monsters, Honda put the boys next door on humming bicycles, the small Honda and Yamaha 90's.

The Twigg, of Twigg Cycles, Inc., explained that the small Japanese machines made it possible for people who were interested in motorcycles to get into the water without getting financially over their heads.

"For a couple of hundred (dollars) up, the people could see what it was all about," Twigg said.

He was reluctant to talk about motorcycle accidents, but he cited inexperience as the chief cause, as in the case of a beginner who tries to hot-rod like a stunt rider.

"It's the ones that are not experienced and think they know it all that get into trouble," he said. "There isn't too much of that though. Young guys pick it up pretty quickly."

Another group trying to improve the public image of the sport is the Antietam Motorcycle Club, whose president, Dan Smith said, "This club doesn't have any 'creeples' in it."

Smith, who is also a radio

Motorcycle Association, which is the chief lobby for the sport.

In addition to policing themselves, the club also sponsors a Little League baseball team, and Smith said it wants to hold classes on safe riding techniques.

"We have a real cross section in our membership," which, he said, includes several members of the city police force, Mack Truck employees, and small business owners. Even the club's official shirt, a blue button - down collar model with the club's name stitched onto the back, looks more like a bowling team shirt than a biker's cos-

Motorcycle clubs, yes, even OMCs, are primarily about sharing one's passions with likeminded people. This is not solely a function of clubs. It is inherent in every gathering of motorcyclists, whether a rally attended by thousands or two guys discovering their shared interest in the grocery store parking lot. At its root, it's the same motivation that drives people to become stalwarts of government, civic and service organizations, and even churches. Motorcycles are not a religion, but for some they aren't far from it.

Outlaw Motorcycles:

To those unfamiliar, there often are certain motorcycles, styles of motorcycles or brands of motorcycles stereotypically associated with the outlaw label. While some clubs do specify that their members own

159

a particular brand or style of motorcycle, the general public frequently has an often-unfounded perception of associating motorcycle type with assumed social behaviors. As with all stereotypes and biases, these perceptions might be founded on some small example. Generally speaking, though as is normal with most unfair stereotypes, this one is unfounded.

The biggest winner *or* loser in this perception game, depending on one's viewpoint, is Harley-Davidson. Harley has long been THE brand of the outlaw genre. Much of this is due to many outlaw clubs holding strong loyalty to the United States. Many trace their roots to returning veterans of WW-II and later wars. Harley of course was the only American motorcycle brand for half of the motorcycle's history. The only brand throughout *all* the period of most OMC popularity building between 1950 and 1990. The brand became *the* choice essentially by default.

For a very long time Harley-Davidson was not happy about this relationship despite it selling motorcycles. In 1967 when Dennis Hopper and Peter Fonda first began preparations to make the film "Easy Rider," as is normal, the film company approached Harley Davidson asking for motorcycles for the project. They were promptly refused. Harley did not want to be associated with the behaviors or the lifestyle depicted by the sample of the movie's plot accompanying the request. The film company resorted to buying used Harley's from a Los Angeles police department auction and having the now iconic choppers custom built by two African Americans, Ben Hardy and Cliff Vaughes. In another ironic and overlooked twist on this *"America"* perception of the movie, Easy Rider actually starts out with the stars riding two European dirt bikes. A (Spanish) Bultaco and a (British) Norton.

I'm quite sure that before its 1969 release, no one anticipated the success the movie would ultimately have. Nor the attractions engendered by it. It was not an Outlaw MC film. It did however associate with many of what had become the standard "outlaw" stereotypes, again largely thanks to Hollywood's exploitation of that film genre. This broad-brush technique applied by the film industry and embraced by the public resulted in a total blurring of any lines between OMC's and motorcycles for many people, but especially Harley-Davidson motorcycles. For many it was the beginning of a new Harley era.

Eventually, Harley-Davidson embraced the image but still, even if only in the background, emphasized their traditional motorcycling dedication. Interestingly, this was also the crowning era of Harley-Davidson's greatest racing history based upon their iconic XR750 race bike design. Times were good for Harley. The quasi-outlaw image eventually became so popular that rather than those true to genuine OMC's, most of the *"bikers"* on America's highways were in-fact dentists, lawyers, bankers, politicians, and even police officers. Professionals, stalwarts of business and government. Harley-Davidson had somehow managed to have their cake and eat it to, and business was very good.

Public perception though can be a fickle thing. Despite knowing their own neighbor is an upstanding, churchgoing, Little League coaching, gentleman, who just happens to ride a Harley-Davidson and wear a leather jacket, when a loud motorcycle passes by, they still envision the *"sub-human deviate"* Bob Maginnis made reference to in trying to dispel that image in his *1972* article. When three or more go by together, people notice. When there are ten, some may even begin to worry. And yet, through all this, the moral, if there was one to Easy Rider, was that it was *Wyatt and Billy's* freedom that was endangered from *normal* people. Such is the irony in taking influence from Hollywood, pop culture, …or social media.

Everyone likes to associate with people who understand their own interests. Maybe it's the sharing of experiences or knowledge. Maybe it's just being accepted. Maybe it's something else. Maybe it's not so much these anthropologically recent machines as it is the ancient *"us vs. them"* tribal instinct that psychologists claim is hardwired into the brains of every human, just waiting for something to be applied to.

Motorcycles though, among users, are a field leveler. The truest *inclusive* activity. Even at the top professional level, it is one of the few professional sports which is not segregated by gender. The all-time winningest competitor in the American Flat Track racing series - single cylinder class, is Shayna Texter-Bauman, a petite, though physically strong, mentally determined, and ferociously competitive young woman. All of her competitors are typically men.

Shayna Texter-Bauman at Hagerstown 2015

At first glance, ethnic minorities seem underrepresented in motorcycling circles. That's another misperception. Closer examination revels that while fewer non-whites are motorcyclists, the per capita attraction to motorcycles is not much different across the artificial boundaries of race. Very simply, *"minorities"* will be less numerous regardless of the subject. That's a mathematical factor, nothing more. The attraction of motorcycles is a human one. None of the unnatural, artificially created categories society likes to cram humans into can change that.

National pro rider, #44 Cameron Smith and the author's grandson, Trevor at Hagerstown Speedway in 2017

*****By the way, Cam *WON* that night!!!!!!!*****

Regional AMA officials 1967

Jack Dugan, Red Moser, Bob Rudy, Shorty Dunford, Billy Bell, Al Wilcox, Dave Warren

Another photo from the 1920's Fairground race depicted in chapter one. It appears from the dust that the photographer missed the bike – again! Everyone is looking to the right of the photo, confirming that the rider just passed by. Note the African American men and boys watching from near the judges stand.

One of several accidents in the first decades of the 20th century attributed to slipping on unfamiliar pavement when most roads were dirt. This one, from <u>June 1913</u>, demonstrates that African Americans (note the period use of *"colored"*) have rode motorcycles for just as long as everyone else.

A motorcycle is simply a machine. Machines do not recognize human characteristics, appearances, economics, physical limitations, or stereotypes. People may vary, but machines are truly equal and offer an extension of that equality to those who use them.

Describing the emotions such as these machines can evoke has been the elusive goal of poets for a millennium. In 1893, Ed Pennington reduced the description to one word, *"Motorcycle."*

Motorcycle Guys

In 1974 Robert Pirsig wrote, *"You look at where you're going and where you are and it never makes sense, but then you look back at where you've been, and a pattern seems to emerge. And if you project forward from that pattern, then sometimes you can come up with something."*

Research can be tough. There are enormous holes in even the best records. Frequently during this project, I had to stop and look back to decide where to go forward. Not so much at the individuals, but at the connecting threads. It is all about relationship. Not blood, but oil. Not family, but motorcycle. And yet, time and again the two were the same. These were everyday people. Just struggling to live their lives. The pattern that eventually emerged was that back then, just as today, they were *motorcycle guys*. They enjoyed having fun. They enjoyed each other's company. There was sort of a loose network among them. I'm no genealogist but they frequently married each other's sisters, aunts, daughters, and nieces. They worked in the same professions. They knew each other. That's common even today. It turns out the motorcycle guys of 1920 had a lot more in common with motorcycle guys in 2020 than either would think. It's not just a latent tribal instinct, it's a tribe.

Not to be overlooked, despite not usually being as visible. Motorcycle guys included, ***and still include*** motorcycle gals as an integral and ever-present part of the story.

What follows is just a random selection of
motorcycle guys over the years

Unknown 1960's Triumph rider

Note the faring to keep loose skirts out of the spokes.

Sandrianna Shipman at Downsville, MD. in 2017

A youthful Marvin Twigg after winning the super-fast Richmond VA. ½ mile. Soon afterward Marvin would begin a long career as a Maryland State Police trooper.

Marvin's brother, Don Twigg at the Daytona 200 1967

Both Twigg brothers raced "Twigg's Cycles" BSA's

Billy Roberts, 1968. Then just a kid in the Frederick, MD ½ mile novice class, riding a 250 Harley-Davison Sprint sponsored by Paul Kitchens & Roy Bowers shop on Cannon Ave. in Hagerstown.

Billy Roberts, the model for the Energizer bunny, still going 46 years later.

171

Don Twigg #31 (2nd) at Dorsey Speedway south of Baltimore 1965

The winner, #9 is Gary Nixon flanked by mechanic Dick Bender and sponsor Bob Myers (holding flag). Bob would be one of 3 founders of AMA Dist.7 the following year and later move to Downsville in Washington County.

Grant Shafer of Sharpsburg being awarded the win with announcer Richard Riley, 2019 All-Star National, Woodstock, VA.

Frank Benson, Herb Reiber and Billy Lloyd "Amateur" [intermediate] class winner, 1st GNC race at Hagerstown, 1964.

Meet the riders' event at the last Grand National Championship race held at Hagerstown Speedway in 2015. Note the gathering clouds. The race would be cancelled later that day by a severe thunderstorm with tornado warning.

1989 Harley-Davidson factory riders & mechanics at the Hagerstown national.

Chris Carr, Mert Lawwill, Jay Springsteen, Bill Warner

Mert Lawwill racing at Hagerstown in 1965 on a Harley-Davidson KR

Travis Taylor, Grant Shafer Sammy Halbert, and Curtis Fisk after a
daylong racing seminar at Downsville, MD. July 3, 2016.

Curtis Fisk, racing Steve Lippoldt's 100-year-old Harley-Davidson at
York, PA. in 2014

Jerry Heil on his immaculate RD350 Yamaha

Jerry Heil [holding bike] with his friend, Hagerstown's Eddie Adkins #58s at the 1974 Frederick, Maryland ½ mile.

National #69 Sam Halbert sharing advice with *Freddie* Sweigert from
Fairplay, MD. and his dad Fred Sr. of Boonsboro.

Joe Howell CB 750f Honda & Gary Moats XS 650 Yamaha, 1975
Photo courtesy Carla Fournier

Mechanic Dick Bender and Gary Nixon at the Hagerstown Speedway

I have many photos of Gary Nixon. Much better ones than the small fuzzy 120 film snapshot this one is from. Probably captured with a fan's Kodak Brownie instead of the German 135 SLR's and 220 Graflex's used by professional and amateur *photographers* at the time. The shot though, captures the moment. I've never seen Dick look so young – or thin. The red-haired Gary, though only 24, already appears older than his years. 1964 would be Nixon's first year to break into the top ten of AMA's national points competition. Four years later he would be grand national champion, for two consecutive years.

Born in Oklahoma, the promising young racer was sponsored in 1962 by a similarly new Maryland dealer and brought east. That sponsor, Bob Myers and his *"Free State Cycles"* we've met already. Nixon would soon become the top rider for Baltimore based Tricor, [Triumph Corporation] then the distributor for every Triumph motorcycle east of the Rocky Mountains. Nixon would make his home near Tricor at Cockeysville for the rest of his life and forever be associated with Maryland motorcycle racing. Inducted into the AMA Hall of Fame in 2003, there are thousands of stories about the "colorful" Nixon. There were many notable *HAGERSTOWN* racers, but Gary Nixon, love him or hate him, was the national image of Maryland racing for decades. Gary died from a heart attack in 2011, his well-known and much-admired wife Mary died during the covid pandemic in 2020.

178

**O. Milton Wilhide (L) telling new owner Donald "Tommy" Thompson
about the 1880 bicycle previously owned by Wilhide.**

Milton Wilhide is included here because he was one of the motorcycle guys. Not a dealer, noted mechanic, racer, or club leader. He was just one of the guys. That's a bit misleading because O. Milton, was never *"just"* anything. Born in 1901, he was a contemporary of Ned Lambert, Chester Delphey, Walt Stoddard, and John Rowland. A professional electrician when electric was still an innovation, he wired Delphey's new store in 1948. Maybe Twigg's to. Many remember him as an usher at St. Mary's church on W. Washington St. He furnished the 1918 photo of the Hagerstown MC in chapter one for the newspaper article it is known from. In a 1954 article he mentioned having owned 23 motorcycles to date. Milton is just one example of the many motorcycle guys through time. The regular riders who made the businesses and the sport a success.

Ned and Ethel Lambert with their 1-year-old daughter, Betty, 1927

Pre-1930 racing.

A primer

Until after World War II, with the noted exception of hill climbing, motorcycle racing essentially meant track racing. Almost entirely, oval track racing. There was some road racing, but conflicts with closing public roads for races or simply racing despite public use soon ended most of it. TT tracks were adopted in 1934 with their left and right turns and required hill essentially as what could be considered the first closed-circuit road-racecourses.

Much has been made of the old board track racing of a century ago. Board track certainly deserves the attention it gets, but too often it overshadows the racing that was taking place at the same time on fairground dirt tracks across the country. The same men, often on the same bikes, made their everyday livings on dirt. The misperception of those who think pro-racing was all about the boards in 1920 would be even more incorrect than another generation somewhere in our future thinking all stock car racing was done on today's dozen or so paved NASCAR tracks. In 1920, essentially every county fairground had a ½ mile or longer racetrack. And every county in the nation had a fairground. Much of the early racing in Maryland is related to a consortium of early Baltimore area motorcycle enthusiasts led by Howard French, who had been a bicycle race promoter before the advent of the gasoline engine. French, and his sons, were among the first motorcycle owners, race promoters and racers in Maryland. Hungry for the sport after Electric Park closed in 1916, but with an injunction by the Maryland horsemen preventing motor racing at Pimlico, the ambitious idea was hatched to go all out and build a motorsport dedicated board track in the Baltimore-Washington metro area.

Baltimore's modernistic "Electric Park," 1914

French, rich on ideas but short on cash for the estimated $500,000 construction cost, began a flurry of dirt track race promotions at every county fairground in the state. The primary focus being to build regional interest and thus, encourage individual investors for the speedway. A portion of the profits from these races was also dedicated to the project as well. Against all odds, French and his associates did manage to secure the hoped-for investors.

In 1924, three-hundred acres was bought at the intersection of Routes 197 and 198 at Laurel and construction of the 1-¼ mile track and facilities soon followed. The racing surface was entirely built of 2"x 4" lumber, bolted together "edge-wise." That's 300 2x4's across the 50-foot-wide track. It was 6,600 feet around. That's more than *123,750 - 16ft. long 2x4's.* And that says nothing of support framing, fencing, the enormous *wooden* grandstands, and the other facilities built to serve 25,000 spectators.

There is a perceived popularity of board track racing. Built near major cities with large populations to draw from, as the official name of **The Baltimore Washington Speedway** implies, Laurel was close enough to draw from two big cities. When considering that potential and the incredible investment of money, materials, and labor to build it, amazingly, it only lasted TWO YEARS.

Starting grid for the inaugural auto race at Laurel in 1924

Racing never resumed after the 1926 season and the facility was soon dismantled. It was not unique in the often-overestimated story of board track racing. There is a photo elsewhere in this book of Chester Delphey and Walt Stoddard with Bill Minnick when Bill won there in 1925.

Most roads were still dirt. In fact, many of the news reports about motorcycle accidents in Hagerstown in the teens and twenties that were not related to collisions are blamed on the tires slipping on smooth cobblestones or the steel trolly rails that ran through many streets.

Dirt was the standard. It was what riders normally rode on. Racing on it was nothing unusual. Board track

Staging for the start of a 1925 bicycle race at Laurel. Interesting to motorcyclists nostalgic for the golden age of flat track racing may be the notation that the most popular brand of racing *bicycle* in 1925 was the British made BSA.

racing is a special element of motorcycle history, but it was special even when it was current.

Some "dirt" tracks were covered with *very fine* gravel or sand. It lessened the weather susceptibility while cushioning the surface for pounding horse hooves. Some horse tracks, especially those used for harness racing still use this treatment. In homage to their horse racing origin, motorcycle racers call them *"cushion tracks."* Occasionally even plain dirt is pulverized into a cushion. Today though, any surface except blacktop is categorically a *"dirt track."*

Motor vehicles of any kind were new and exciting before 1920. In 1909 when the very first race was staged on the brand-new Indianapolis Speedway, rather than cars, it was a motorcycle race held by the F.A.M. Modeled on the famed Brookland's track in England and specifically designed for motor racing, the new track had been "paved" with *coarse* crushed stone. The surface would cause the race to be cancelled before completion due to dire safety concerns. While the modern design made it frighteningly fast, the new surface gave even less predictable grip than the familiar dirt in the corners and the coarse stones shredded the early, soft rubber tires resulting in sudden and unpredictable, control robbing blowouts.

The numerous resulting crashes with virtually no safety gear but a leather cap and heavy wool jersey, produced contusions, abrasions, and lacerations from head to toe as riders tumbled over the sharp-edged stones. One news report compared the surface to a cheese grater. The races though, drew an enormous number of people

The commercial potential of that aspect for hotels, restaurants, stores, and other establishments was not lost on businessmen in cities across America and soon, every city wanted to stage a professional motorcycle race. And every county had a fairground racetrack.

Except for local amateur races occasionally held for bragging rights or trophies, this was "Class A" racing. Professional riders who did this for their living, riding special race-only bikes. Early on, there were essentially no rules. During the brief period of the F.A.M., safety rules were adopted at the larger sanctioned events. Small local races though were still largely at the promoter's discretion. Helmets were a very early requirement. Although originally, they were nothing but a lightly padded leather skull cap.

Unbelievably today, the second-generation helmets, the so called, *"hard shelled"* replacements of leather caps, were made by soaking canvas and cardboard in varnish or shellac and molding it over a form in paper mâché fashion. The very first fiberglass helmet wasn't made until the mid-50's and Bell Helmets introduced the first full-face unit in the 60's. Neither development saw rapid acceptance by the riders who they were designed to protect. Open faced helmets were still quite common on racetracks into the mid-1970's. The earliest full faced versions do look like a bucket with a slit in the front, adding some credence to the typical complaint of it restricting vision.

Early on, leather trousers were adopted, later followed by a leather jacket and still later, the two pieces attached to form a full suit. Double layers were added at key impact points such as knees, shoulders, and elbows, sometimes with meager padding. These "leathers" have remained the standard race wear to the present. It has only been in the last few years that computer operated air bags have been integrated into the lining of the suits to provide more than simple abrasion protection. Only the top pro riders can afford such expensive gear. Most (track) racers still wear leathers that are little changed from those of 100 years ago.

Amazingly to me, one of the last elements of gear to become common is gloves. In any fall, whether from a motorcycle or tripping over your own feet it is just instinct to extend the hands to catch yourself. Crashing a motorcycle usually offers little chance of your hands being much good in *preventing* injury, but few have the presence of mind to consider that in the split second before you hit the ground. Instinct kicks in and the hands go out… if there's even time for that. Yet, even into the 1980's racer photos are occasionally seen without gloves.

The dozens of small motorcycle factories in 1920 essentially built every bike one at a time anyway. Building a special race bike for class A racing only entailed bolting on the unique go-fast bits hoped to make it better than the rest of the competition. Those bits were frequently built as one-offs as well.

Unknown pre-1930 dirt track race. Indian 1ˢᵗ (L) H-D 2ⁿᵈ & 3ʳᵈ.

This wasn't *just* about competition and being number one. There is a familiar old saying in racing circles that *"what wins on Sunday, sells on Monday."* Brand loyalty is often built and reinforced at the track. For the factories, it was primarily about sales. But it was also about innovation. At that time in history, the racetracks of America were basically the R&D testing facilities of every motor vehicle manufacturer. The meteoric advances in automotive technology that took place between 1900 and 1930 are mostly due to developments to win races. But it wasn't just about making a faster machine! Many developments came about to simplify the often complicated or delicate machinery. Many of those developments were aimed at making parts more simple, fewer, more resilient, lighter, and generally better.

All class A racing was done on these special one-of-a-kind *"works bikes."* One part deemed unnecessary, which race bikes still generally lack today, is a starter.

Fuel also adds weight and often, it was carefully measured so that only *just* enough for the prescribed number of laps was carried. Of course, this was an estimate. In October 1919, an unfortunate rider with a wide easy lead in the 100-mile race on the big two-mile board track in Sheepshead Bay, Brooklyn, N.Y. ran out of gas ½ mile from the finish line. It earned him the lasting nickname, *"Hard Luck Nixon."*

The above photo is obviously not from 1920. It was made at the Barbara Fritchie Classic in 2015. The Fritchie has been held annually on July 4th in Frederick Maryland since 1921. This was a special one-time race – and it *was* a real race – staged among a group of antique motorcycle enthusiasts. Every bike in the race is an original, built before 1924.

Period staging before the start. Note that each rider is attended by an assistant to push-start him. Typically, the rider's mechanic, it is a tradition that continues to present in flat track racing. Although a remote electric powered starter temporarily held to the side of the engine is the usual means of starting today. In very recent years, advances in electronics have even made it possible to produce onboard electric starters and batteries to operate them light enough to be incorporated into weight conscious race engines. But they are still the exception.

Another accessory that was deemed unnecessary on early race bikes was brakes! The goal after all, was to go and go fast. Brakes only slow you down!

Surprisingly to many, brakes were not **_allowed_** on racing motorcycles until 1969. Even then, many protested the change fearing that it would actually decrease safety when riders suddenly slowed in front of a following bike, and cause rear-end collisions.

Less scary than it sounds, the rider had a "kill switch" button on the handlebar that would cut the electric necessary to fire the spark plugs. Thus, he literally shut off his engine to slow down. Restoring power while the bike was still moving turned the rear wheel by the retained momentum and restarted the engine. This was a *sort-of* brake as the momentum of the bike was retarded by having to turn the wheel and thus move the pistons against their compression. Essentially it was an engine brake as still utilized in a very modified form on big trucks. That's that loud **_BRAAAAAP_** sound you hear when passing a truck descending a mountain. Halting the bike at the finish line or pits often required "Flintstones" style foot action.

Neither did the engines have oil inside them as we think of that critical necessity today. Oil was constantly dripped into the applicable parts from a remote tank by a manually operated oil pump the rider had to remember to activate regularly. The excess used oil, after doing its job in the engine was allowed to simply drip out the bottom.

Yet, by as early as 1910, class A race bikes were using engines even larger than those allowed for racing today. For the 2022 season, "**American Flat Track**" the operator of the pro series, increased the maximum displacement of race engines to 900cc but the standard, as it has been since WW-II, remains 750cc. In a previous chapter it is noted that 93-years-ago, Walter Stoddard's *average* lap time on a mile track was only ten seconds off the *fastest* lap in the Oklahoma mile in 2021.

Jared Mees (*sponsored by Twigg's Cycles!)* won that 2021 race on a state-of-the-art Indian FTR750 with all the latest computer assisted design and tuning the modern world possesses. He did it wearing a personally tailored leather suit with computer operated airbag technology that can sense when he is in distress and deploy in the fraction of a second before, he hits the ground. He wore a special impact resistant helmet and countless other items of safety gear with multiple ALS paramedics *and* a dedicated surgeon standing by. Just in case.

Walt Stoddard made his record setting run on a stripped down 1,000cc Harley-Davidson race bike with no brakes and the same cheesy tires people used on the street in 1930. His safety gear consisted of a leather cap, *glass* goggles, a pair of leather trousers and a thick wool Harley-Davidson jersey. His boots were no different from those worn by farmers or railroad men. He had no gloves.

If there was a crash, and there always were, if the rider couldn't get up on his own and walk away, a doctor from the nearby town might be summoned to come to the track with whatever equipment and medicine he carried in his small bag. Sometimes, if the rider had someone to do it, he might be loaded into a car and taken to a hospital, *if* there was one nearby.

Ray Weishaar, the Harley-Davidson factory rider many recognize from the popular photo of him sharing a Coke with his pet piglet after winning the 1920 Marion Indiana, road race, crashed through a fence at Ascot speedway in Los Angeles California in 1924. Ray did walk away initially dismissing the incident. Just one more of many crashes he'd had during his career. But his wife insisted on driving him to the hospital, just to be checked out.

Ray died there four hours later from undetected internal bleeding. Top Indian factory star Gene Walker would die a similar death on a dirt track on the other side of the country at Stroudsburg, Pennsylvania just ten-weeks later.

Spectator safety rules were once a bit laxer as well.

Washington D.C. rider Freddy Fretwell after winning the
Alexandria VA. race. This single cylinder Harley is a ½-mile race
bike. In 1926 AMA briefly restricted engines to 21 cubic inches
(350cc) on tracks shorter than 1-mile in an attempt to reduce
speeds and the many high profile racing incidents that were then
regularly occurring. Note the manual syringe-style oil pump on the
side of the tank.

Postscript

History is nothing but the collective story of each person's contribution. Our lives are brief. Sometimes exceedingly and unfairly so. They are too numerous to chronicle outside our own small spheres. For the unremarkable, the normal people, each one's unique story is usually limited to the memories of those who knew them. The stories may live on among family and friends for a generation or two, but seldom more. Yet, each one, even the briefest life, has played some small role in the larger drama… of *history*,

This book was spontaneous. Unplanned. I've always saved snippets of motorcycle history but several years ago, attracted by one photo of a motorcycle, I bought an old photo album at auction and busy with other projects, put it away. One day I took it out and realized it was from Hagerstown. Eventually, I discovered that all the photos in it were motorcycle related. They were even better than motorcycles. They were the motorcycle people of the past and I wanted to know them.

Every search resulted in more new questions than answers. It led far from the initial evidence that triggered it. Each lead suggested more. More people, more places, more connections, and experiences. Obscure overlooked links emerged. Random scraps began knitting back together and making sense as a larger, more complete fabric.

I had to share their story. It was almost lost. Much of it still is. The world will survive without them, but their contributions deserve recognition. *They* deserve to be remembered. Both the celebrated *and* the unknown.

Many voids remain but this story exposes the connections within generations, and across them. Connections spanning many imagined and perceived barriers made less so because of it. The connection is an enigma. A solitarily operated machine demanding self-confidence. And yet, it unites people. The world could use a lot more self-reliance and unity.

The times, the people and the motorcycles have changed, but the camaraderie, the attraction, and the connection are the same. This is for them.

The Motorcycle guys.

One and all. Past and present.

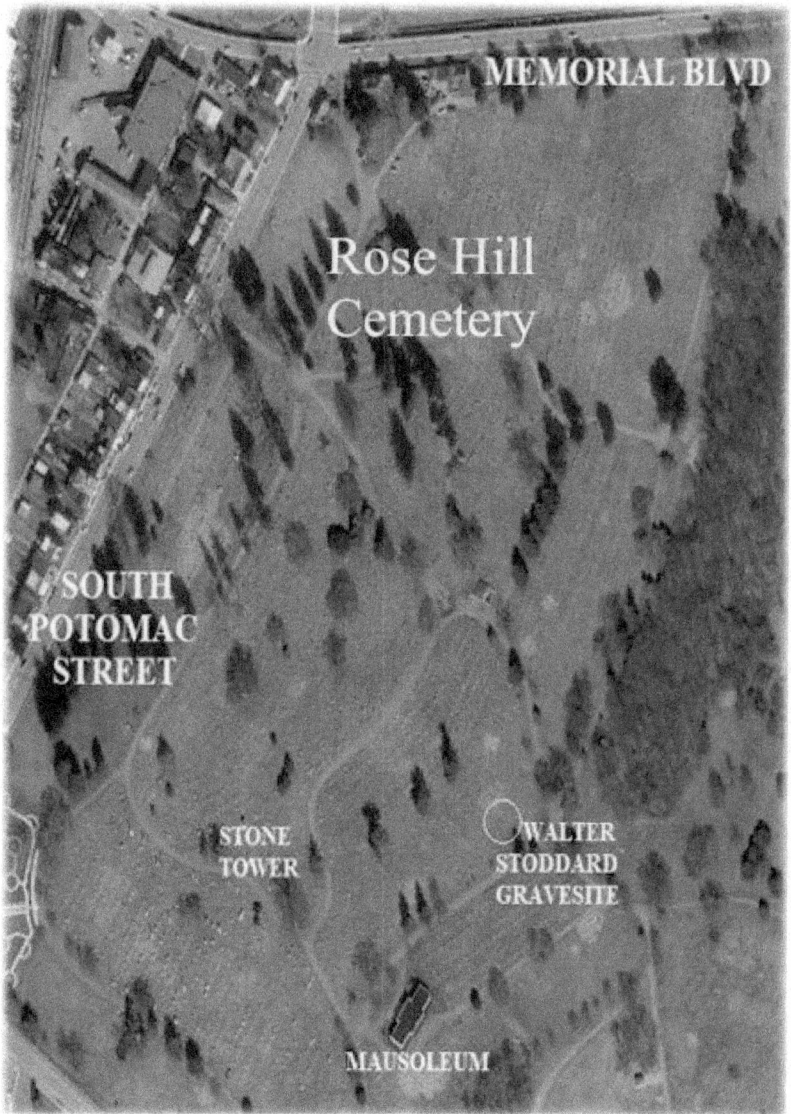

MEMORIAL BLVD

Rose Hill
Cemetery

SOUTH
POTOMAC
STREET

STONE
TOWER

WALTER
STODDARD
GRAVESITE

MAUSOLEUM

A genuine friend,

who lived and cherished motorsport history

Rich Keadle

1962 – 2021

If you enjoyed this little book, you may also like **100 Years of Flat Track Racing, The Barbara Fritchie Classic, Frederick, Maryland**.

Over 400 pages and more than 380 illustrations. Many of them rare or unpublished. It is essentially the story of motorcycles in neighboring Frederick County leading up to and throughout the history of the race that has been held annually since 1921 on the same Frederick Fairgrounds track where it still runs every July 4th. It is the oldest continuously running motorcycle race *anywhere*. 100 Years of Flat Track Racing is likewise available from Amazon.com and some local sellers.

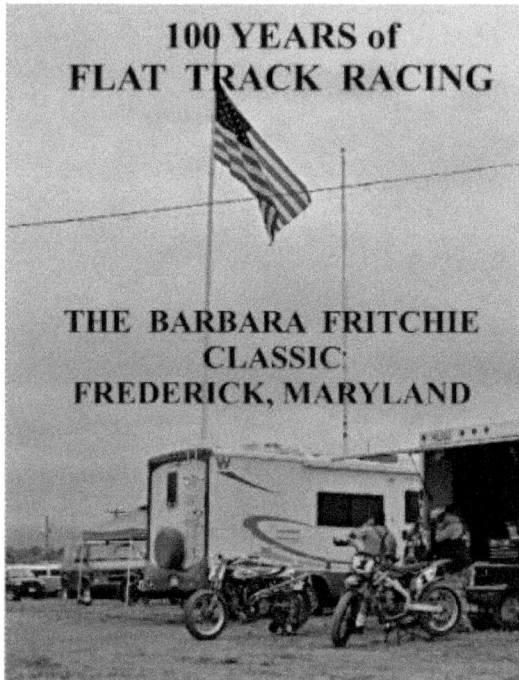

100 YEARS of
FLAT TRACK RACING

THE BARBARA FRITCHIE
CLASSIC:
FREDERICK, MARYLAND